*At dusk weeping
comes for the night;
but at the dawn
there is rejoicing.*

PSALM 30:5

A CHRISTIAN PERSPECTIVE
ON PAIN AND SUFFERING

With the dawn
rejoicing

MELANNIE SVOBODA, SND

TWENTY
THIRD 23rd
PUBLICATIONS
www.23rdpublications.com

NOVALIS

To Kathleen Hine, SND
and Tim Shepard, SJ
for all the times
you hastened the dawn
in my life

Twenty-Third Publications
A Division of Bayard
One Montauk Avenue, Suite 200
New London, CT 06320
(860) 437-3012 or (800) 321-0411
www.23rdpublications.com

The Scripture passages contained herein are from the *New Revised Standard Version of the Bible*, copyright ©1989, by the Division of Christian Education of the National Council of Churches in the U.S.A. All rights reserved.

ISBN 978-1-58595-699-9
Library of Congress Catalog Card Number: 2008925360

Printed in the U.S.A.

Published in Canada by Novalis, Saint Paul University, Ottawa, Canada

Business Offices:
Novalis Publishing Inc.
10 Lower Spadina Avenue, Suite 400
Toronto, Ontario, Canada
M5V 2Z2
Phone: 1-800-387-7164
Fax: 1-800-204-4140
E-mail: books@novalis.ca
www.novalis.ca

Novalis Publishing Inc.
4475 Frontenac Street
Montreal, Quebec, Canada
H2H 2S2

ISBN 978-2-89646-084-7

Cataloguing in Publication is available from Library and Archives Canada.

We acknowledge the financial support of the Government of Canada through the Book Publishing Industry Development Program (BPIDP) for our publishing activities.

Contents

❧ Introduction ❧

Recently I was diagnosed with polymyositis, a rare disease where the autoimmune system begins to attack and destroy healthy cells in the body. Its symptoms include painful swelling, general muscle weakness, and chronic fatigue. There is no known cause for polymyositis and no cure. Twenty percent of the people who get it die within five years. Others are able to manage the disease through medication.

About the same time I learned I had this chronic illness, I had just written a book entitled *When the Rain Speaks: Celebrating God's Presence in Nature*. When a friend learned of my illness, she said, "Melannie, you should write a book called *When the* Pain *Speaks*." This is that book.

Millions of us experience pain in our lives, whether it is physical, mental, or emotional. At times our pain is minor: a sore muscle, worry over rising prices, a disagreement with a friend. Other times our pain is major: crippling arthritis, looming financial disaster, the severing of a cherished relationship. No matter its form or intensity, pain interrupts our life. It takes us aback. It forces us to ask questions like: Why did this happen to me? Did I do something bad to deserve this? What should I do now? Where is God in all of this?

This book provides help for people dealing with pain—any kind of pain. It offers thirty-six meditations on various aspects of pain and suffering. Rooted in our Christian faith, the chapters explore topics such as: the universality of pain, pain as wise advisor, Jesus the healer, dealing with setbacks, befriending the imperfect, pain and laughter, the suffering of the saints, biblical images of suffering, and death and resurrection. Each chapter begins with an engaging quotation from a wide variety of sources. The quotation is followed by a meditation on the topic and an appropriate prayer. Each chapter concludes with a question or two for personal reflection as well as a suggested action for the day.

That great Christian writer C.S. Lewis once said, "God speaks to us in our joy; God shouts to us in our pain." I tend to agree with him although perhaps he exaggerated the volume of God's voice. The Jewish writer Martin Buber said that God addresses us continuously via a silent presence that infuses all of creation. Buber referred to this unique communication of God as "silent thunderings." The truth is, sometimes God shouts to us in our pain, yes, but sometimes God whispers too or even thunders silently. But the fact remains, as we journey through life, God is speaking to us always—in our sorrows and joys, disappointments and successes, our fears and hopes. And yes, God speaks to us in our pain in a special way. It is my hope that this book will be a helpful guide for your listening.

❧ 1 ❧

Where Is Your Pain?

*In life as in dance: Grace glides on
blistered feet.*   ❧ ALICE ABRAMS

Where is your pain? Perhaps you can answer that question right away because your pain is very real and obvious: you are suffering from a chronic illness, you have lost a loved one, you are a victim of abuse, you received some bad news from your doctor, or you just experienced a major setback or disappointment.

Or maybe you are feeling pretty good right now and would describe your life as relatively pain free. Even if you are not currently experiencing any major pain in your life, you certainly have experienced pain in the past. You know quite well what pain is. And

3

you are probably realistic enough to know that you will experience pain again in the future. Most of us can subscribe to the words of Uncle Remus: "You can't run away from trouble. There ain't no place that far."

None of us lives a pain-free life. That's the first thing to remember about pain: It is universal. Pain knows no age limit. A two-year-old knows what pain is and so does a 102-year-old. Pain knows no gender. Both men and women suffer pain. Pain is not restricted to any economic, political, or social class. A wealthy businessman in Saudi Arabia knows pain as well as an impoverished seamstress in Bangladesh, an octogenarian grandmother in Denmark as well as a twenty-five-year-old taxi driver in South Korea. Pain speaks every language. It enters every home. It invades every heart.

Because pain is universal, it has the potential for uniting all human beings. The English historian Henry Hallam said, "Pain is the deepest thing we have in nature, and union through pain has always seemed more real and holy than any other." The woman in Atlanta who has just lost a child weeps when she sees the woman in Darfur rocking her dead baby on TV. They are one in their pain. Pain can unite even so-called enemies. On the news I saw a World War II veteran from the United States meeting by chance a World War II veteran from Japan. When the two men realized they had fought against each other in the Pacific in 1944, they both wept and then embraced. Their shared experience of the hell of war made them one. Yes, pain can be holy, for it has the power to unite us as nothing else can—not even joy.

Pain can break down barriers between you and me, him and her, us and them. If we took time to really know other people—especially those we think of as our enemies—and if we really probed their hearts, we would (in the words of the poet Henry Wadsworth Longfellow) "find in each life sorrow and suffering enough to disarm any hostility."

> *Loving God,*
> *help me to name my pain,*
> *whether it is major or minor,*
> *current or past, obvious or hidden.*
> *Renew my realization that*
> *all human beings suffer pain*
> *regardless of age, gender, race, religion,*
> *or economic status.*
> *May I use my own pain to break down barriers*
> *between myself and others.*
> *May my realization of other people's pain,*
> *disarm any hostility I may have in my heart.*
> *I ask for these graces through Jesus*
> *and the power of his life-giving Spirit. Amen.*

Reflection

Where is my pain? Has my pain ever united me with another? If so, when and how?

Action

I will reverence the pain—spoken or unspoken—of every single person I meet today.

❧ 2 ❧

The Mystery of Pain

There are no answers to some of the great pressing questions. You continue to live them out making your life a worthy expression of leaning into the light.

❧ Barry Lopez

Some things in life don't make sense. We call these things mysteries. Bumblebees are a scientific mystery. According to scientists, bumblebees shouldn't be able to fly—aerodynamically speaking—and yet they do. There are historic mysteries too. Whatever happened to the Lost Colony? Then there are the everyday mysteries: Why do I do some of the stupid things I do? Why does my spouse/child/friend/sibling act in that annoying way? Yes, these are mysteries. But the greatest of all mysteries is the mystery of human pain and suffering.

Not all pain is a mystery, however. Some of it makes sense. If you accidentally put your finger into a fire, the pain will force you to jerk your finger out—thus preventing a serious burn. If you over-eat, you are apt to get indigestion. No mystery there. But other pain makes no sense at all. Why must that five-year-old have to undergo painful chemotherapy? Why did those two God-fearing parents have to lose their only child to a drunk driver? Why did that earth-quake have to hit that country already reeling under widespread economic impoverishment? It just doesn't make sense.

From ancient times, religions have tried to make sense of pain and suffering in an attempt to answer the most difficult question of all: Why do the innocent suffer? In Hinduism, suffering is seen as a karmic debt owed from a previous incarnation. Through our pain we build up good karma to balance out the bad. For Buddhists, suffering is the consequence of desire—especially inordinate de-sires. Extinguish all desire, and extinguish all suffering. In Rabbini-cal Judaism, suffering is seen either as something willed by God or as a consequence of human disobedience to God's commands. In Islam, suffering is viewed as the result of Allah's positive will: "Ver-ily We have created man into toil and struggle" (*Koran* 90:4).

We Christians don't have all the answers to the mystery of suf-fering. But we do have Jesus. We believe that in the person of Jesus, God took on human flesh. He ate our food, drank our water, and walked our roads for about thirty-three years. Because he was fully human, Jesus experienced suffering. So we will begin to explore the mystery of suffering by considering Jesus. The English writer J.R.R.

Tolkien, author of *The Lord of the Rings,* said this about the story of Jesus: "There is no tale ever told that people would rather find is true." Let's look at that story.

God of Mystery,
I know that some pain makes sense.
It alerts us to danger,
      it warns us of trouble.
Other pain is the consequence of bad choices.
But much pain does not make sense.
When I see the innocent suffering,
      I find myself asking again and again,
         "How could a good God allow this to happen?"
Give me patience to probe the mystery of pain.
Let the wisdom of the various faith traditions
      speak to me.
And may I always keep in the forefront
      of my probing
the beautiful story of Jesus, your Son,
      who knew firsthand
both the joy and pain of being human. Amen.

✍ Reflection

Have I ever asked, "How could a good God allow this to happen?" If so, what was my answer?

✍ Action

I will ask God for the grace to probe the mystery of suffering.

∾ 3 ∾

Jesus:
God Wrapped
in a Person

*If you want to get across an idea, wrap it
in a person.*   ∾ RALPH BUNCHE

We Christians believe that God entered human his-
tory in the person of Jesus Christ. Tradition tells us
he was born in a stable and slept in a manger, a feed-
ing trough. At the age of one or so, his parents were forced to flee
with him into Egypt to escape King Herod's awful decree to slay
all the young boys in his realm. When it was safe, they returned
to Palestine, a small Jewish nation dominated by a foreign power,

the mighty Roman Empire. They settled in Nazareth, a small hick town, where Jesus lived in obscurity, probably learning his father's trade of carpentry.

When Jesus was about thirty, he had a profound religious experience that radically altered his life. He left the security of his home town and became an itinerant preacher. Living a poor and simple life, he relied on the support of friends for his public ministry. Though he was initially very popular with the crowds, he soon encountered opposition from certain religious leaders. His enemies labeled him a glutton, a blasphemer, a demon. They threw him out of the synagogue and threatened him with stoning. Even members of his own family thought he had lost his mind.

In the end, Jesus was betrayed by one of his closest friends and handed over to the Roman authorities. While almost all of his friends deserted him, Jesus was tried unjustly and sentenced to death. He was mocked, flogged, beaten, and forced to carry a heavy wooden cross to Calvary. There he was nailed to the cross where he hung for three agonizing hours before he finally died.

As we undergo the trials of daily living, we must keep before us the person of Jesus. Because he was fully human, he suffered just as you and I suffer. He knew the pain of ordinary life: loneliness, hard work, boredom, misunderstanding, inconvenience, disappointment, uncertainty, confusion, fatigue, and loss. And he knew the extraordinary pain of terror, betrayal, abandonment, prolonged physical agony, and death. In Jesus, God does not ask us to suffer what he himself has not experienced in one form or another. When we are in pain, let us bring our pain to Jesus, for he understands. He *really* understands.

Philosopher Peter Kreeft has said it well: "There is one good reason for not believing in God: evil. And God himself has answered this objection not in words but in deeds and in tears. Jesus is the tears of God."

Suffering Jesus,
I believe you are fully divine and fully human.
During your thirty-three years on earth
you experienced the joys and pains
        of ordinary human life.
I bring my pain to you today,
knowing full well that you understand my pain
        even more than I do.
Help me to bear this pain as you bore yours:
        not necessarily with complete understanding,
but always with courage
        and absolute trust in God. Amen.

✍ Reflection

What pain of Jesus speaks most to me at this time in my life? Why?

✍ Action

Today I will take my pain to Jesus, for he understands.

4

Pain and Sin

I always say that pain is information; it is not punishment. — Susan Taylor

Some pain is caused by the choices we make. If we eat too many beans, for example, we may get the pain of gas. If we drive recklessly, we may end up with the pain of an accident or a ticket. If we don't invest time in our relationships, we may experience the pain of loneliness. Other pain is caused by sin. Innocent people are slaughtered because of a demagogue's lust for power. Wars are waged because of a nation's greed for gold or oil.

But some people take this idea further and say that all pain is our fault. Or all pain is a punishment for our sin. They say things like this: "You had that heart attack because you don't go to church" or

"I got cancer because I've been a lousy parent" or "That city was devastated by the hurricane because it's filled with evil casinos." This belief that there is always a direct link between pain and sin has been around for a long, long time. It was rampant even during Jesus' time.

One day Jesus and his disciples meet a man blind from birth (John 9:1–7). The disciples ask Jesus, "Rabbi, who sinned, this man or his parents, that he was born blind?" Notice, the disciples automatically assume that the man's blindness is caused by sin. They're just not sure whose sin caused it. But Jesus makes it clear that this man's blindness is not the result of anyone's sin when he says, "Neither this man nor his parents sinned." Then he adds something interesting: It is "so that God's works might be revealed in him."

When we experience pain in our lives we too might be tempted to think we did something wrong to deserve this pain. If that line of thinking were true, however, then all virtuous people would have pain-free lives. But we know that's not true. All we have to do is look at the lives of the saints. For all the saints, despite their diversity, have one thing in common: They suffered, some of them terribly so. (See the chapter on "Suffering and the Saints.")

If we are tempted to say that our pain is a direct punishment for our sins, let's remember what Jesus said about that line of reasoning. Let's recall his words to his disciples. And let's hear him say these words to us, "Your pain is not caused by your sin. Trust me on this." Then hear him add, "But the works of God can be made visible through you and your pain." And let's ask him to show us how they can.

Jesus, help me to see that my pain or illness
*   is not a punishment for any sin.*
Pain happens. Accidents occur.
Illness is a part of life.
Help me to face my pain squarely
*   and to discern the information*
*   it has to offer me:*
*   to trust you more deeply,*
*   to rely on others more humbly,*
*   to face each new day with courage and hope.*
May the works of God
*   be made more visible in me and in my pain.*
*   Amen.*

✍ Reflection

Am I ever tempted to view pain as a direct
punishment for sin? If so, what can help me to
resist this temptation?

✍ Action

I will find one way for the works of God to be
made visible in me today.

❧ 5 ❧

Jesus as Healer

Jesus went throughout Galilee, teaching in their synagogues and proclaiming the good news of the kingdom, and curing every disease and every sickness among the people. ❧ MATTHEW 4:23

All four gospels are filled with stories of Jesus as healer. He cures Peter's mother-in-law, a man with a withered hand, a woman bent over for eighteen years, a man born blind, a woman suffering from a hemorrhage, a paralytic, a man possessed by demons, ten lepers—and the list goes on. Sickness and pain aroused in Jesus a profound compassion. On more than one occasion the gospels say that "his heart was moved with pity" (Mark 6:34).

Jesus cures people—sometimes asking only for an expression of their faith. To the father of a boy possessed by a demon, Jesus says, "All things can be done for one who believes" (Mark 9:23). Other times he seems powerless not to cure people—faith or no faith. He cures the man with a withered hand, for example, and the woman bent over for eighteen years even though neither of them had even requested a cure (Mark 3:1–6; Luke 13:10–17). Sometimes Jesus says that the physical healing he bestows is but a sign of a deeper spiritual healing that has taken place—for example, when he cures the paralytic who was lowered through the roof (Mark 2:1–12).

But as we follow Jesus' public life, we notice something. The closer he gets to Calvary, the more infrequent the healings become. Once a veritable river, the miraculous cures eventually become a mere trickle. What's going on here? Was Jesus' compassion drying up? Was he losing some of his power? Not really. Scripture scholars explain this peculiar phenomenon in this way. As Jesus grew in understanding of his mission, he realized he was sent not to take away people's physical pain and suffering—though he could. Rather he was sent to embrace human pain and suffering himself and thus teach us that they can be redemptive. What's more, in the words of Paul Claudel, "Jesus came not to eradicate our pain, but to fill it with his presence."

All the people Jesus cured eventually died of something. Even the three individuals he raised from the dead—Jairus' daughter, the son of the widow of Naim, his good friend Lazarus—all died again. Clearly preserving physical health and extending earthly life were not the goals of Jesus' mission. But accompanying us in our pain, suffering, and death is.

This doesn't mean we shouldn't pray for the physical healing of ourselves or others. After all, our faith encourages us to ask for the things we feel we need. And, amazingly, healing miracles still occur. But we must always bear in mind that people's spiritual health is far more important than their physical health. And eternal life far outweighs this earthly life. Furthermore, in the person of Jesus we have a friend who not only fully understands our pain, but who wants to share it with us. Are we willing to let him do that?

Jesus, you are a healer.
Come and heal me of those physical pains
*   that get in the way of my love for you and others.*
If this is not possible or wise in your eyes,
*   then help me to use my pain*
*   as an impetus to greater compassion for others.*
Lead me to see that all pain can be redemptive.
Strengthen my belief that as wonderful as this
*   earthly life can be,*
it pales in comparison to the heavenly life
*   you have prepared for us from all eternity.*
Jesus, fill all the corners of my life with your
*   presence. Amen.*

✍ Reflection

What healing story in the gospels touches me the most? Why?

✍ Action

I will prayerfully read one of the healing stories from the gospel today.

❧ 6 ❧

The Sufferings of Jesus

*Jesus asserted that, despite suffering,
despite injustice, despite misery, and
despite death, everything would still be
all right in the end. Because his Father
was love.* ❧ FATHER ANDREW GREELEY

In his book *So We Do Not Lose Heart*, Father Demetrius Dumm, OSB, writes: "The greatest paradox of Christianity is the equal emphasis placed on both the cross and the resurrection." He explains that both of these realities are essential to our understanding of who Jesus is. Without the resurrection, says Dumm, "the cross is a terrible disappointment." Without the cross, "the resurrection is pure fantasy."

The cross reminds us that our hope of resurrection is grounded in the reality of pain and suffering. The resurrection tells is that the cross of our suffering and our earthly existence will end in glory: fullness of life in heaven forever. When we are experiencing pain, however, we tend to focus on the cross and sufferings of Jesus. That's understandable. I would like to say a few things about the sufferings that Jesus endured during his passion.

Books have been written about Jesus' passion, some of them describing in minute detail the sufferings he underwent for us: the mockery, the beatings, the crowning of thorns, the torn flesh, the loss of blood, the agonizing thirst, the nailing to the cross, the sense of abandonment, the struggle just to breathe, the prolonged death. There is no doubt that Jesus experienced excruciating pain. What a consolation this is for any of us who has suffered in any way—whether we were ridiculed, beaten, subjected to painful tests or treatments, had difficulty breathing, or felt abandoned by everyone, including God. When we are in agony, we know that Jesus has been there before us. He knows what pain is. He understands what we are going through.

But Jesus did more than merely experience human pain. He transformed it. By offering his pain for others—for you and for me—he filled even senseless pain with meaning. And that meaning is love, unconditional love. Jesus was totally innocent, yet he willingly accepted his passion and death out of love for us—all of us. In this way he models what we can do with our pain. We can unite it with Jesus' suffering and endure it out of love for others. Jesus' pain, as well as our pain, has little meaning without this unconditional love.

The cross and the resurrection. Suffering and loving. Fr. Demetrius summarizes it well in these words: "The suffering of Jesus was intense, but it was not his suffering that saved the world; it was his loving."

Jesus,
*   help me to embrace the great paradox*
*   of my faith:*
*   the equal emphasis it places*
*   on the cross and the resurrection.*
*   Lead me to see that without the resurrection*
*   the cross is " a terrible disappointment."*
*   And without the cross,*
*   the resurrection is "pure fantasy."*
*   When I am experiencing any kind of pain,*
*   help me to remember the agony you experienced*
*   on Calvary.*
*   You have been where I am.*
*   You know what I'm going through.*
*   You understand.*
*   But most of all, Jesus,*
*   may I always remember the great love*
*   that gave meaning to your pain.*
*   For I truly believe: It was not your suffering*
*   that saved the world,*
*   it was your loving. Amen.*

✍ Reflection

Do I tend to emphasize the cross or the resurrection in my personal spiritual life? Or do I place equal emphasis on both?

✍ Action

I will read the passion of Jesus and see what aspect speaks most to me today.

❦ 7 ❦

The Resurrection of Jesus

Hope…is our human power of bridging what is yet humanly unbridged, of believing what is not yet seen, of seeing what is not yet visible.

❦ Sister Joan Puls, OSF

For Christians, any discussion about pain or suffering must be anchored in the resurrection of Jesus, that earth-shaking event that is the cornerstone of our faith. In this chapter we will look briefly at three facets of the resurrection of Jesus.

First of all, we Christians believe the resurrection actually happened. All four gospels insist: The tomb was empty. Jesus was raised from the dead and appeared to scores of witnesses. This belief in the resurrection formed the heart of the early apostolic preaching (Acts 2:2, 4:10). Writing to the Corinthians, some of whom were denying that Jesus rose from the dead, St. Paul says, "If Christ has not been raised, then empty too is our preaching; empty, too, your faith" (1 Corinthians 15:14).

We also believe the resurrection was not an event for Jesus alone. We believe the resurrection of Jesus guarantees the resurrection of all of us. Jesus died. Jesus rose. But he takes all of us with him. For us, death is not a terrifying passage into darkness; it is a glorious transition into eternal light. But we don't need to wait until death to receive the power of the resurrection. That same power is given to us now, working in and through us to transform the world. Reverend Simon Perry explains this well: "If we believe in the resurrection, our hope is invested not only in a God who will bring us through death to live in his presence, but in a God whose living presence transforms our present living."

Because of the resurrection of Jesus we have hope. We Christians do not deny the pain and evil in our world—and, indeed, in our own hearts. We know there are countless reasons for despair as we behold the widespread evil in and around us: violence, war, greed, addictions, corruption, and injustices of all kinds. Yes, we see these evils; but we see *more* than these evils. We see the promise given to us by the resurrection of Jesus: "He will wipe every tear from their eyes, and there shall be no more death or mourning, wailing or pain, for the old order has passed away"

(Revelation 21:4). Only people who believe in the empty tomb could hang on to hope amid the gloom and despair of contemporary times. And only hope could sustain us in our efforts to bring about that new order proclaimed in Revelation, an order of justice, peace, and love.

Thomas Groome, theology professor at Boston College, summarizes the impact of the resurrection in these words: "No oppression can hold us bound, no evil can finally triumph, no trouble can rob us of hope, no sin can enslave us, no dependency is beyond recovery, no hurt is beyond healing—if we truly believe that 'Christ is risen, risen indeed.'"

Risen Jesus,
  strengthen my belief in your resurrection
    from the dead.
Help me to see that your resurrection
    guarantees my resurrection into eternal life.
May I come to believe that the power
    of your resurrection
    is available to me not only at my death;
It is available to me now, this very day.
May my belief in the resurrection increase
    my hope.
And may my hope sustain my efforts
    to bring about a new order of justice,
    peace, and love. Amen.

✍ Reflection

How does my belief in the resurrection of Jesus impact my attitude toward death? toward pain and suffering?

✍ Action

I will cultivate hope today.

8

Pain as Wise Advisor

There is no coming to consciousness without pain. ⮜ CARL JUNG

We tend to look upon pain as an enemy. Our instinctive response is to get rid of it. So we take drugs to dull our pain. We seek distractions. We live in denial. But rather than view pain as something intrinsically negative, we can choose to see it as something potentially positive. For the truth is, pain can be a wise advisor.

How? Spiritual writer Anthony de Mello, SJ, a wise man himself, wrote, "Suffering is given to you that you might open your eyes to the truth." I experienced this when word got out to my religious community about my illness. Soon afterwards I received hundreds of cards, notes, and emails from Sisters of Notre Dame all over the world expressing their concern and promising their prayers. I was overwhelmed by this outpouring of support. Because of my illness, because of my pain, my eyes were opened to these truths: How thoughtful my sisters really are, how important prayer is to them and to me, and how much I was loved by them.

Yes, pain is a wise advisor who can help us see the truth more clearly. What kinds of truth? The truth that every single day is precious. The truth that our loved ones mean more to us than we imagine. The truth that we need to give and receive love to be happy. The truth that other people can be incredibly generous. The truth that we are not in control of our destiny. The truth that we can't go it alone. The truth that we desperately need God.

If pain is a wise advisor, then it behooves us to listen to our pain. How might we do this? One way I have found helpful is to dialogue with my pain as I would dialogue with a real person. Sometimes I even write out the dialogue in my journal. You can begin by simply asking your pain, "What are you telling me?" or "Do you have some wisdom to share with me?" Then listen to what your wise advisor has to say. You might hear things like this: "Let go...Slow down...spend more time with your family...check your priorities again...talk to God more...be patient...take one day at a time...enlarge your world...count your blessings...reach out to her...forgive him already...love."

Is pain, your wise advisor, trying to tell you something? Shhh! Listen!

Wise God,
help me to see my pain as potentially positive.
Let my pain be a wise advisor for me
   who opens my eyes to the truth:
      the value of each day,
      the immeasurable worth of my loved ones,
      the goodness of other people,
      my absolute need for you.
Help me to dialogue with my pain
   and listen to the wisdom this wise advisor
   has to share with me.
Then please give me the grace to act
   from the wisdom I've gained through my pain.
   Amen.

✍ Reflection

Have I ever learned any wisdom from my pain?

✍ Action

I will dialogue with my pain today—either a current pain or a past one—to learn from this wise advisor.

❧ 9 ❧

A World without Pain

Nothing great was ever done without much enduring. ❧ St. Catherine of Siena

When we are experiencing pain, it is easy for us to long for a world without pain. Imagine, a world with no toothaches, no misunderstandings, no cancer, no uncertainty, no loneliness, no killing, no terrorism, no wars. At first glance, it sounds like it would be a pretty wonderful place. But if we delve deeper, we might see that there is often a direct link between pain and understanding, and between suffering and love.

Malcolm Muggeridge, the great British journalist and Christian apologist, said he would not want a world devoid of pain. In his later years, Muggeridge maintained that everything he had learned that truly enhanced his existence had been learned through suffering. He concluded, "If it were possible to eliminate affliction from our earthly existence by means of some drug or other medical mumbo-jumbo, the results would not be to make life delectable, but to make it banal and trivial to endure."

This is not to say that pain is good. Quite the contrary. Much of the pain in our world is the direct result of people's evil choices, choices flowing from pride, greed, hatred, lust, and selfishness. We are called to work toward the alleviation of this type of pain. Other pain results from accidents, incurable diseases, and natural disasters, all parts of the human condition. Once again, we are called to respond to this suffering with love and compassion. Yet, as Muggeridge implies, even these afflictions can be our teachers.

Pope Benedict XVI, when he was a Cardinal, was asked what he thought about ridding the world of suffering. He said, "Anyone who really wanted to get rid of suffering would have to get rid of love before anything else, because there can be no love without suffering." Why is this so? He explains: "Because love always demands an element of self-sacrifice." And self-sacrifice "will always bring with it renunciation and pain."

A few examples might help here. Why do we experience so much pain when a loved one dies? Precisely because he or she was our *loved* one. The pain of our grief is the direct result of our love for that individual. Why are we in anguish when we see our grown children, grandchildren, or other family members making poor choices? Because we worry about them, because we love them. Why do we willingly make great sacrifices for a friend, our family, our local community, our country? Because of the love we have for these entities.

A pain-free world sounds heavenly. But a world devoid of love would be hell.

> *Loving God,*
> *when I am experiencing pain,*
> *and I long for a pain-free world,*
> *help me to recall that much of my pain is wedded*
>   *to my love.*
> *I love, therefore I care. I care, therefore I hurt.*
> *I love, therefore I make willing sacrifices.*
> *Lead me to see that loving always demands self-*
>   *sacrifice,*
> *and self-sacrifice always involves a certain amount*
>   *of suffering.*
> *Give me the grace to embrace the pain*
> *that is the direct result of my loving*
> *just as Jesus embraced the pain of the cross*
> *out of his great love for us. Amen.*

✍ Reflection

What pain have I experienced that was the direct result of my loving?

✍ Action

I will make a willing sacrifice out of love today.

10

The Parable of the Good Samaritan

Compassion is the willing disposition to enter into the chaos of another.

— James Keenan

The parable of the Good Samaritan is a parable about pain. It is also a parable about compassion, the loving response to pain. As such, it serves as a model for anyone who has ever cared for another in pain. We're probably familiar with the story. A Jewish man sets out from Jerusalem for Jericho. Along the way he is attacked by hoodlums who beat him, rob him, and leave him half dead on the side of the road.

A priest happens by, sees the man, and, for whatever reason, passes by. A Levite also comes along but he doesn't stop either. Perhaps they both thought the man was already dead. Or maybe they had urgent business elsewhere. Or, as some Scripture scholars maintain, maybe they were strictly observing the purity laws of their religion, which forbade them to touch a corpse lest they become unclean. We dare not judge these two men too harshly, for, if we're honest with ourselves, we know that we too have come up with some pretty reasonable, creative, and even pious reasons for not helping others.

But then a Samaritan, a natural enemy of Jews, happens by. Moved with compassion at the sight of the man, he stops. Bending down, he dresses the man's wounds, pouring his own oil and wine onto them. He carefully hoists the man onto his own animal and takes him to an inn where he continues to care for him. The next day he pays the innkeeper to continue to nurse the man, promising to stop in again on his way back.

As we travel through life, we too come across individuals lying in pain along the side of the road. Perhaps they are victims of crime, war, famine, or abuse. Or maybe they are struggling with a terminal illness or the debilitating effects of old age. Then again they may be suffering from dementia, a personality disorder, a broken heart. Whatever the cause, they are in pain. And we, seeing them, are moved by compassion to help. Putting aside our own agenda, we listen to them, we pour the oil of understanding onto their wounds, we assist in moving them forward along the road, and we solicit the aid of others for their healing.

The Samaritan in Jesus' parable is an icon of goodness not because he is pious, austere, or orthodox. He is good because he is compassionate. It is compassion that gives us a keen sense of our solidarity with all human beings. It says, despite all that separates us, we are one. The survival of the human race—and the planet itself—depends on compassion.

Jesus, I love your parable of the Good Samaritan.
It touches my heart very deeply.
Help me to imitate this incredibly compassionate
*   man.*
Help me to notice and respond
*   to people in pain along the side of the*
*   road of life.*
Teach me to put aside my own plans,
*   to listen to their stories,*
*   to use what little I have to treat their wounds.*
Help me to move them forward
*   and to solicit the help of others if needed.*
And may I, once and for all,
*   get rid of my reasonable, creative,*
*   and pious excuses*
*   for not being a more compassionate person.*
The survival of humankind and planet earth
*   depends on it. Amen.*

✍ Reflection

Have I ever been a Good Samaritan for someone?
Has someone ever been a Good Samaritan for me?

✍ Action

I will willingly go out of my way to help someone
today.

❧ 11 ❧

Slowing Down

*For fast-acting relief from stress, try
slowing down.*   ❧ LILY TOMLIN

O
ne thing pain does is this: It slows us down. A sore an-
kle makes us hobble along rather than run full speed
ahead. Swollen hands take more time to button shirts
or open jars. Being forced to slow down by pain can be frustrating.
But the truth is, sometimes slowing down isn't such a bad thing
after all.

We live in a world where speed and efficiency are virtually wor-
shiped. Multitasking, e.g., doing several tasks at the same time, is
now considered normal behavior. More than that, it is actually
demanded in the workplace where productivity often determines

whether you keep your job or not. Against such a backdrop, slowing down may seem like an unrealistic option.

Granted, there will be times in our lives when we will be extremely busy. There will be days when we will be forced to rush around. Yet, I believe, even amid the most hectic of times we can still carve out a few moments each day when we deliberately slow down not merely to smell the roses, but also to taste the strawberries, to pay attention to the people we live or work with, to think things through, to take stock of our priorities, and to talk to God. I believe if we don't do this on a regular basis, we run the risk of becoming physically ill, of jeopardizing our relationships, of slipping into despondency, or of losing our way altogether.

Slowing down can reconnect us to the larger matrix of life—especially the world of nature. Such reconnecting can be spiritually nourishing. Once there was a woman who had had a difficult life. In 1937 she married a farmer who turned out to be an alcoholic. Almost single-handedly she raised their four children, often working into the night and not knowing how she was going to pay the next bill. Yet through it all she found time to write beautiful letters to her sister in another state, not bemoaning her hard lot, but describing the lilac bush in spring, the birth of the new calf in summer, the brilliant colors of the leaves in fall, the sound of the howling wind in winter.

Years later, the woman's daughter, upon finding the letters, came to this realization. Her mother was able to endure the hardships of her hectic life precisely because she stayed connected to the wider world of creation. In the recurring seasons of nature—spring, summer, fall, winter—she found nourishment for her own inward life, a life marked by birth, growth, diminishment, death, and new birth again. This consistent nourishment gave her the strength to go on despite her busyness and burdens.

Slowing down can reconnect us to the larger matrix of life. Slowing down can save us.

> *Slow me down, God.*
> *Help me to smell the roses, taste the strawberries,*
> *pay attention the people I live and work with,*
> *think things through, take stock of my priorities,*
> *and (most importantly) talk with you.*
> *Keep me connected to the larger matrix of life,*
> *to the natural world in which I live,*
> *with its recurring and consoling seasons.*
> *Slow me down, God.*
> *I ask for this grace through Jesus your Son*
> *who walked gently, slowly,*
> *and deliberately upon our earth. Amen.*

Reflection

Is there any evidence in my life that I worship the gods of speed and efficiency? Have I ever been forced to slow down because of pain?

Action

I will slow down at some point today and reconnect with the large matrix of life.

⚜ 12 ⚜

Thank God for Difficult People

Whenever evil befalls us, we ought to ask ourselves, after the first suffering, how we can turn it into good. So shall we take occasion, from one bitter root, to raise perhaps many flowers. ⚜ LEIGH HUNT

Pain is not good. Yes, it can alert us to go see the doctor. Yes, it can warn us to slow down, eat less, and tend to our relationships. But pain is never a good unto itself. Pain is (excuse the pun) a pain.

But, as we have seen, pain does have its benefits, its blessings. In Sanskirt, the word for pain is *vedana*, a word that means not only suffering but also knowledge. Pain is a means by which we gain knowledge—about ourselves (I am not invincible), about others (she is very generous), about humanity (we all want essentially the same thing for our children and grandchildren), about the world (we are all crew members on spaceship earth), and even God ("God is a mystery wrapped in a mystery wrapped in a mystery," wrote Thomas Merton, the Trappist monk.)

Pain also has the power to mold and form us as few things can—even our greatest joys. In her book *Spirituality for Dummies*, Sharon Janis says this: "Trials are tools that pry you loose from a smaller world view and push you—even running and screaming—into more precious realms that you may not have known existed." Pain can give us a broader perspective on life. It can take us places we may never have gone had it not been for pain's gentle nudging or powerful shove.

Pain can also bring forth good qualities in us. Mark Rosen has written a book whose title captures this concept: *Thank You for Being Such a Pain: Spiritual Guidance for Dealing with Difficult People*. The basic premise of the book is this: Although congenial people are wonderful to live and work with, they do not elicit as much virtue from us as difficult people do. Difficult people (sometimes we call them a pain in the neck!) help form us into better human beings, because they call forth from us an array of beautiful virtues such as patience, understanding, compassion, humility, courage, and generosity. (We may think we are always congenial, but we too are probably eliciting virtues from other people right now!)

We should not seek pain. We should not ask for it. But when it comes—especially through difficult people—we are invited to look long and hard at our pain, this bitter root, and find the flowers it has to bestow.

God of Mystery,
I know pain is not good, in and of itself.
But I also know pain can bestow certain benefits,
*   even blessings.*
May my pain pry me loose from my smaller
*   world view*
and take me to more precious realms
*   I didn't even know existed.*
May my pain—
*   especially the pain of dealing with difficult*
*   people—*
mold and form me into a better human being,
*   a more virtuous one.*
I ask for these gifts
*   through Jesus who bore his pains*
*   with patience, humility, and great, great love.*
*   Amen.*

✍ Reflection

What knowledge have I gained through my pain?
How do difficult people elicit virtues from me?

✍ Action

I will look long and hard at my pain today and find
one blessing, one flower, it has to bestow on me.

❧ 13 ❧

Learning the "New Normal"

The trick is what one emphasizes. We either make ourselves miserable or we make ourselves happy. The amount of work is the same. ❧ CARLOS CASTANEDA

I n the early stages of my illness, I became very frustrated. "I don't know how to behave," I told a friend. "Sometimes I think I'm babying myself and other times I think I'm being too hard on myself." My friend shared something that she had learned in a class on chronic illness. When people are first diagnosed with a chronic illness, they have to learn a "new normal."

What was normal for them before the onset of the illness will no longer be normal for them now. My friend added, "I think that's part of your frustration. Right now you don't know what your new normal looks like. You're still collecting the data."

My friend's words have helped me bear pain and frustration with greater equanimity. Now when my ankles swell up, for example, rather than getting fearful or frustrated, I have learned to say, "Swollen ankles are now part of my new normal." When I become tired and need to take a nap in the afternoon, rather than bemoaning the fact that I didn't used to have to take a nap, I tell myself that a nap is just part of my "new normal."

I think the concept of "new normal" is helpful for anyone undergoing a major change in life. The birth of the first baby affects a couple's normal life drastically, as they try to discover a "new normal" that now includes a wailing baby. The death of a loved one also disrupts a person's normal life in a profound way. Part of the grieving process is learning to find a "new normal" that now includes the absence of someone who was a very significant part of our previously normal life. Moving to a new place also disturbs our normal life as we are forced to establish new routines, meet new people, and get to know a whole new geographic area.

The simple aging process constantly challenges us to discover a "new normal" as well. When my mother was well into her 80s and living alone, I remember her saying to me with a laugh, "I used to work fifteen minutes and rest five. Now I work five and rest fifteen!" She had found her "new normal."

Learning the "new normal" takes patience and humility. Accepting it becomes easier if we remember that God is with us no matter what our normal looks like.

> *Loving God,*
> *help me to see that any major change in my life*
>   *challenges me to learn a new way of seeing*
>   *and a new way of being in the world.*
> *Give me the grace to find my "new normal."*
> *And give me patience to collect the data I need*
>   *to discover what that "new normal" looks like.*
> *And when the time comes,*
>   *give me the courage to bless and let go of the*
>   *"old normal"*
> *and to welcome and embrace the new.*
> *Keep reminding me that you are with me*
>   *no matter what my normal looks like. Amen.*

✍ Reflection
What current changes in my life are calling me to learn a "new normal"?

✍ Action
I will practice patience and humility today.

14

Befriending the Imperfect

Usefulness is not impaired by imperfection. You can still drink from a chipped cup. ⟩ GRETA K. NAGEL

In a perfect world there would be no pain. Everyone would be in perfect health. Everyone would get along with everybody else all the time. All buses, trains, and airplanes would run on time. And there would be no need for jails, airbags, or erasers. But we don't live in a perfect world. Pain reminds us daily of our own imperfection and the imperfection of others and the world around us. Most of us have accepted the imperfection of the world with our heads. But some of us have not really accepted it with our hearts.

You've heard of personal trainers, I'm sure. These are professional men and women who force other people to jog, do sit-ups, drink carrot juice, and eat flaxseed—and they get paid big bucks for doing it. Well, inside many of us dwells someone I like to call our Personal Critic (PC for short). Like a coercive personal trainer, our PC demands that we be perfect and he (or she) chastises us severely when we are not. When we look in the mirror, for example, PC says things like this: "You're fat...You're bald...Your teeth are crooked...You had two chins yesterday. Today you have three!" If we do something good—like cook dinner for twelve, shoot a 72 in golf, lose ten pounds, or even raise a family—PC will whisper in our ear, "Not good enough!" If nineteen out of twenty people write positive comments about a presentation we gave, PC will focus our attention on the one negative comment—so much so that we forget altogether what the other nineteen wrote!

If we could silence our Personal Critic we would minimize some of the unnecessary pain we experience by trying to live up to his or her unrealistic demands. How can we silence our PC? We begin by befriending—with mind and heart—the imperfect world in which we live. Roses have thorns, cars break down, friends disappoint. Befriend them anyway. We must also accept our own imperfections. We accept the nose we're stuck with, our tendency toward impatience, and the fact that we can't do it all. We know that although we are striving to become a better human being, there are some faults we will carry with us to our grave. And guess what? That's okay! As someone once said, "Practice makes better. Only Jesus is perfect."

Yes, befriending the imperfect can ease some of our pain. (My Personal Critic just told me this chapter wasn't good enough, but I told him to back off!)

Omnipotent God,
help me to silence the tyrannical voice
    of my Personal Critic
who constantly whispers in my ear,
    "Not good enough! Not good enough!"
Give me the grace to befriend the imperfect
    in myself, in others, and in the world
        around me.
Remind me that I will carry some of my faults
    with me
        to the grave—and that's okay.
Keep calling me to become not a perfect person,
    but a better one.
I ask these graces through Jesus
    who had a fondness for imperfect people
    like me. Amen.

✍ Reflection

Do I have a Personal Critic inside of me? If so,
what kinds of things does he or she say? How do I
silence my PC?

✍ Action

I will not listen to my Personal Critic today. And
I will not be someone else's Personal Critic today
either.

❧ 15 ❧

Pain and Laughter

If you want to forget all your other troubles, wear tight shoes. ❧ ANONYMOUS

Have you heard any of these? The early bird gets the worm, but the second mouse gets the cheese...A car mechanic said to a customer, "I couldn't fix your brakes, so I made your horn louder."... Good intentions and crying babies should be carried out quickly... A woman prayed, "Lead me not into temptation. I can find the way myself." When we are in pain, it is difficult to smile and laugh. Temporarily, we may lose our sense of humor completely. That's understandable. But the operative word is *temporarily*. What makes pain more bearable is if we can laugh on a regular basis even amid our tears.

When I was first diagnosed with polymyositis, my hands and feet were painfully swollen. Consequently I had a hard time doing even simple tasks such as brushing my teeth, combing my hair, and getting dressed. At first I was frustrated and upset. But gradually, I began to see some humor in my situation. One morning I tried, with considerable difficulty, to put on my new pair of thick elastic stockings. I sat on the edge of my bed and tugged and tugged on them. Soon I was rolling all over my bed still trying to pull them on. Suddenly I thought, "If the world could see me now!" The thought made me laugh out loud. Another time I was slowly creeping up the stairs, pausing on every step. I said to my deceased mother who died at age 90, "Hey, Mom! I'm looking more like you every day—only I'm 25 years younger than you were when you looked like this!" I immediately sensed my mother was smiling down upon me.

Psychologist Ellie Katz has said these wise words: "Warning: Humor may be hazardous to your illness." That's because humor helps us to keep things in perspective. It reminds us that we are human. Only human. At the same time, it reminds us that we are not the center of the universe. The world does not revolve around our hurt feelings or our latest toe surgery. When we laugh, we are acknowledging the wider context in which we live, a context that includes pain, yes, but also the love of other human beings and our gracious God. Humor also tells us that we are more than our pain. Pain does not determine who we are. Only love does.

What are some ways we can hang on to our sense of humor even when we are in pain? First, we can associate with humorous people. We can tell our friends we need to lighten up and give them permission to make us laugh. We can also make it a practice to read the comics every day or invest in a good joke book. Or how about renting a funny movie and watching it with some friends? And finally, we can simply ask God for the grace of a sense of humor. We ask God for all kinds of other graces, why not ask for this one that will help us bear our pain with greater composure and calm?

And finally, I like what the 85-year-old woman said: "Just because I have pain doesn't mean I have to *be* a pain."

Loving God,
when I am in pain,
    it is hard for me to smile and laugh.
But if I lose my sense of humor
    may the loss be only temporary.
I ask today for the grace of a sense of humor.
Help me to see some humor in my current
    situation.
Remind me to keep things in perspective,
    to accept my humanness,
and to be in touch with the world beyond
    my illness or pain.
I ask for this grace through Jesus,
    our Smiling Redeemer. Amen.

✿ Reflection

How important is my sense of humor to me? Why?
What helps me to keep it alive?

✿ Action

I will nourish my sense of humor in some way
today.

❧ 16 ❧

Mary and the
Pain of Uncertainty

*Faith means living with uncertainty—
feeling your way through life, letting your
heart guide you like a lantern in the
night.*   ❧ DAN MILLMAN

O ne of the pains I suffer with polymyositis is the pain of
uncertainty. When I was first diagnosed, I went online
to find out all I could about this little-known disease.
When I learned that 20% of the people with this condition die
within five years, I wondered, how many more years do I have?
What condition will I be in? Polymyositis is characterized by pe-

riodic flare-ups. In my ministry of giving talks and retreats, I have to schedule myself a year or two in advance. How can I promise to give a retreat a year from now when I don't even know how I'm going to be feeling tomorrow?

Uncertainty is a peculiar kind of suffering. That's because most of us want to know what tomorrow is going to bring—so we can be prepared. We like to plan ahead too. Planning helps us to feel we're in control of our destiny. But the uncertainty of living—especially if we are beset with chronic illness—won't give us that luxury. As John Lennon said, "Life is what happens to you while you're busy making other plans."

Mary, Jesus' mother, experienced the pain of uncertainty in a notable way. As a young girl, she had made plans for her life. She was going to marry Joseph and live a quiet life in obscure, little Nazareth. But God, through an angel named Gabriel, broke into her world and radically altered her plans by asking her to bear Jesus, the Son of the Most High. Her consent to God was exemplary and complete: "May it be done to me according to your word" (Luke 1:38). But her "yes" also created wholesale uncertainty for her. What was she going to tell Joseph? How would he react? How would the two of them raise a child destined to be the Messiah? What would her son's life be like? Some of Mary's uncertainties are recorded in Scripture: the birth in Bethlehem, the flight into Egypt, the loss of Jesus in the temple, his itinerant life, his growing unpopularity, his arrest, passion, and death. Mary endured the uncertainties of life with both humility and patience. She "pondered" these uncertainties, eventually entrusting all to the God she had come to know as good and gracious.

In her book, *When the Heart Speaks,* author Sue Monk Kidd says this about the blessing of uncertainty: "Growth germinates not in tent dwelling but in upheaval. Yet the seduction is always security rather than venturing, instant knowing rather than deliberate waiting." Like Mary, may we ponder the uncertainties of our life in prayer. Then may we venture forth or deliberately wait, knowing that God is with us, calling us to ever greater growth.

> *Mary, Mother of Jesus,*
> *you experienced the pain of uncertainty.*
> *Your "yes" to God at the Annunciation*
> *didn't bring you security;*
> *it brought you upheaval instead.*
> *You knew the uncertainty of giving birth*
> *in Bethlehem,*
> *fleeing into Egypt,*
> *and losing your young son in Jerusalem.*
> *Later, you experienced the uncertainty*
> *of Jesus' ministry,*
> *his arrest, passion, and death.*
> *Help me to deal with the uncertainties of my life—*
> *uncertainties associated with illness,*
> *relationships,*
> *employment,*
> *religious beliefs,*
> *aging,*

political issues,
local problems,
global peace.
In the midst of these uncertainties
lead me to ponder, to pray,
trusting in the God I know as good and gracious,
a God calling me to ever greater growth. Amen.

Reflection

What are some of the uncertainties in life that I am dealing with right now? How can the example of Mary be a source of encouragement for me?

Action

I will ponder one uncertainty today and see how God may be calling me to greater growth.

17

The Pain of Conversion

Change is the nursery of music, joy, life, and eternity.
— John Donne

One major source of pain in our life is change. Although we may think we are flexible and adaptable, the truth is many of us have a natural suspicion of and aversion to change. We prefer things to stay pretty much the way they are, thank you. Sometimes we even prefer a bad situation that we know to a potentially better one that we don't know, simply because we are afraid of making a change. Sadly, many abused women choose to stay in an abusive relationship, because making a change is just too daunting.

Sometimes we also equate change with weakness. We label politicians "wishy-washy," for example, who change their minds about some issue. But is that fair? The great leader of India, Mahatma Gandhi, was known for often changing his mind publicly. One aide asked him how he could contradict today something he had said last week. Gandhi replied, "Because this week I know better." Change, rather than indicating weakness, often signifies growth. And, as Gail Sheehy has said, "Growth demands a temporary surrender of security." That's scary. That's painful.

The deepest kind of change we can make is called conversion. Theologian Bernard Lonergan defines conversion as "a change in course or direction." We are traveling in this direction in life, but then something happens—we gain a new insight, we suffer a major trauma, we experience a great joy—and now we are going in a new direction. Sometimes the change is only a degree or two; other times it is a veritable u-turn.

Authentic conversion demands a letting go. But it is more than a letting go of something we can easily afford to lose—like the coins in our pocket or the color of our hair. Rather, conversion is a letting go of *who we are*. It means letting go of our attitudes, habits, personal preferences, ways of thinking, or pet dreams—those things we equate with our very identity as a person.

In Scripture the Greek word for this type of conversion is *metanoia*. Literally it means a change of heart. But pastor/writer Robert Stoudt describes the depth of *metanoia* in these words: it means "to be split apart and reknit back together again." Ouch! Jesus' memorable image of conversion is a grain of wheat breaking up in the ground. But remember: the splitting apart, the dying, is not an end. On the contrary, it is the beginning of abundant new life. That is the promise inherent in conversion's pain.

Conversion doesn't happen overnight. It takes time. It is not easy either. Conversion demands great courage. Little wonder writer Paul Wilkes calls conversion "incremental heroism."

Loving God,
Sometimes I welcome change, sometimes I don't.
Sometimes change is just too hard,
 too daunting,
 too scary.
Help me to navigate the many changes in my life.
Help me to grow,
 to change direction,
 to change my heart.
When I am split apart by change,
 reknit me back together again.
When I feel like that grain of wheat dying
 in the ground,
 remind me that such dying leads to
 abundant new life.
I ask this through Jesus, who was
 split apart on Calvary
 and rose to new life on Easter morning. Amen.

℘ Reflection

What changes are easy for me? Which are difficult? What makes the difference?

℘ Action

Today I will be attentive to any calls for conversion—both small and large.

❧ 18 ❧

The Suffering of the Saints

Saints are…simply superlative versions of the rest of the family. ❧ GEORGE HUNT, SJ

As I said earlier, all the saints have one thing in common: they suffered. But when we hear stories of saints being eaten by lions or thrown into caldrons of boiling oil, we think, "That's probably not going to happen to me." Sometimes the sufferings of the saints can seem irrelevant to our lives. But if we look more closely, we see that many of the saints endured sufferings similar to those experienced by many people in our own day. Here are a few saints and some particular sufferings they endured.

St. Catherine of Siena (1347-1380): She didn't get along with her mother her whole life.

St. Marcella (325-404): When she was 85, robbers broken into her home and beat her.

St. Celestine V (1209-1296): This pope abdicated the papacy because he felt his gifts were not a good match for the job; the next pope, out of jealousy, threw him in prison where he died.

St. Germaine Cousin (1579-1602): As a child, she was abused by her father and stepmother.

St. Mary Queen of Scotland (1046-1093): Her husband and son were killed in war.

St. Elizabeth of Portugal (1271-1336): Her husband was a playboy.

St. Joseph Pegratelli (1737-1811): He was kicked out of his native country, Spain.

St. Monica (323-387): For 30 years she anguished over the amoral living of her eldest son, Augustine.

St. Malchus (4th century): He contemplated suicide.

St. Rose of Lima (1586-1617): She suffered from frequent illness.

St. Catherine of Genoa (1447-1510): She married a man with whom she had nothing in common, suffered chronic depression, and experienced bankruptcy.

St. Jeanne de Chantal (1572-1641): She lost three children in infancy, her husband in a hunting accident, and her only son in war.

St. Hugh (1140-1200): He refused to pay taxes that would be used for the Crusades and suffered severe consequences.

St. Francis of Assisi (1182-1226): He was a POW for over a year.

St. Julie Billiart (1751-1816): She was paralyzed for 22 years.

St. Benedict Joseph Labre (1748-1783): He was a homeless beggar most of his life.

St. John of the Cross (1542-1591): He was betrayed by his friends.

Swedish historian Nathan Soderblum says, "Saints are persons who make it easier for others to believe in God." They do this by their example. They suffered as we do, and yet they continued to trust in God—as we are striving to do. Their example inspires us more than any theological treatise could.

God of all,
the saints had this one thing in common:
  they suffered.
Some of them suffered extraordinary pain:
    extreme asceticism,
      terrible torture,
      gruesome deaths.
But others endured sufferings more similar to
  my own:
    sickness,
    family problems,
    misunderstandings,
    the death of loved ones,
    financial insecurity,
    psychological problems,
    worry,
    abuse,
    betrayal.
The saints had the courage to live the faith
  in their time, place, and circumstances.
May I find the same courage to live the faith
  in mine.
Despite their sufferings,
  the saints proclaimed
  your goodness and love.
Give me the grace to follow in their steps. Amen.

Reflection

Are there any saints that I am particularly drawn to? Why?

Action

I will read up on at least one saint today.

❧ 19 ❧

The Pain of Messiness

When order crumbles, Mystery rises.

❧ JOHN SHEA

I was talking with a friend who was experiencing some major challenges at work. After describing her complicated situation, she blurted out, "I just want things to be neat!" Then she added, "I guess I have a hard time with messiness."

Messiness can be painful—even on an everyday practical level. No matter how organized we are, dust accumulates, laundry piles up, car keys get mislaid, pets shed, rooms get cluttered, kids create mayhem. But messiness exists on deeper levels too. We want things to go one way and they go another way. We want a relationship, for example, to run smoothly, and instead it chugs, sputters, and grinds to a halt. We want a loved one to be happy, and he is depressed or she is pouting. We want our parish or workplace to be a place where everyone gets along, and we see bickering and petty jealousies instead.

Life is not neat. But Jesus never said, "Come, follow me and you will have a neat little life...All your relationships will be in order... All your endeavors, tidy." Instead he said things like this: "Take up your cross and follow me" (Mark 8:34)... "Do you think I have come to establish peace on earth? No, I tell you, but rather division" (Luke 12:51)... "I am sending you like lambs among wolves" (Luke 10:3–4).

What can we do to live more graciously with a certain amount of messiness of our lives?

First, we can remind ourselves that too much neatness is not good. It can actually stifle life. I know this from my experience as a writer. I am ordinarily a neat person. But when I'm writing an article or a book, my office is a mess. There are papers strewn all over the floor, note cards piled high on my desk, and books falling off my bookshelves. I've learned that this kind of messiness, though a scandal to "neatniks," actually breeds creativity. It sparks ideas. It brings forth life. Therefore I not only accept it, I welcome it.

We can also remind ourselves that there are more important values in life than neatness and order, such as generosity, kindness, thoughtfulness, humor, wonder, gratitude, forgiveness, and joy— to name a few. If these values are alive and well in ourselves, our homes, our workplaces, our parishes, then a little bit of messiness is no big deal. Years ago one of our sisters was dying of cancer. She was only 38. I had just been made novice director, so I asked her one day, "What advice would you give me in my work with the novices?" Without hesitating she said, "Less emphasis on house-cleaning and more emphasis on how to get along with others."

God of order as well as chaos,
I like things to be neat—ordinarily.
I like things to go the way I want them to go,
    the way I've planned.
When I experience the messiness of life,
    give me patience.
Help me to see that too much neatness,
    too much control, may actually stifle life and
    creativity.
Keep reminding me that there are
    other values in life
    far more important than neatness and order—
        like kindness,
            humor,
            wonder,
            and joy.
I ask for this grace through Jesus who experienced
    the chaos of living, the chaos of death,
    and the chaos of resurrection. Amen.

✍ Reflection

How am I currently experiencing messiness in my life? What helps me to live graciously with a certain amount of messiness?

✍ Action

I will nourish one value in my life today that is more important than neatness.

20

When Pain Comes as Darkness

Our whole business in this life is to restore to health the eyes of the heart, whereby God may be seen.

St. Augustine

When pain comes as darkness, I may be flooded with emotions such as confusion, anxiety, fear, loneliness, helplessness. Perhaps I myself turned out the light by something I did or didn't do. Maybe I'm the one who blew out the candle or stepped across the threshold into the night. Or maybe the darkness was imposed upon me. Maybe it overtook me so gradually I didn't realize it was coming, or so suddenly I was thrown off balance. Whatever the cause or the timing, here I am, enveloped in darkness.

My first impulse might be to fight against the absence of light. I may frantically grope for a switch or some matches. I may cry out for help. I may take a few faltering steps forward. But if nobody comes and the ground is uneven and the darkness persists, I might just have to sit down and wait it out.

I know if I am patient, my eyes will gradually adjust to the darkness and I will begin to see at least a couple of shadows. And that usually happens. Soon I can detect a few outlines of familiar shapes even though most of my known world is still unrecognizable. I think how quick we are to equate darkness with evil and light with goodness. But I know that's unfair. Goodness is bred from darkness, while some evils are committed in broad daylight. So I begin to appreciate the goodness darkness can bring.

Like new life, like birth. The seed in the ground germinates in the dark. The baby develops in the night of the womb. Darkness is also the milieu for intimacy, sleep, and healing. In the darkness my other senses come alive—especially my hearing and my touch. And if I wait long enough, I soon sense that Someone is with me in the night. I recall with great consolation that my God is not only the God of blazing light, but also the God of pitch darkness. As the psalmist says, "Darkness is not dark to you; the night is as bright as day, for darkness is as light to you" (Psalm 139:12). Betsie Ten Boom wrote this from the pitch darkness of a Nazi concentration camp: "There is no pit so deep that God is not deeper still." There is no darkness so impenetrable that God cannot be found in it.

God of Light and Darkness,
be with me always, all ways,
whether I am walking confidently in the light
or groping anxiously in the darkness.
When I am in darkness,
give me patience to appreciate
the wisdom and goodness the night
might have to offer me.
Give me the faith to trust that you yourself
are with me in the darkness.
I ask this through Jesus who knew
the pitch darkness of Good Friday
as well as the blazing light of Easter morning.
Amen.

✒ Reflection

At a time when I experienced darkness, how did I feel? What did I do? Did the darkness bestow any goodness or wisdom upon me?

✒ Action

I will be patient with any darkness in my life right now, trusting that God is with me in it.

❧ 21 ❧

When We Feel
Like Job

*I have come to understand that there are
two kinds of faith. One says if and the
other though. One says: "If everything
goes well, if my life is prosperous, if no
one I love dies, then I will believe in
God...." The other says though: "Though
the cause of evil prosper, though I sweat
in Gethsemane, though I must drink my
cup at Calvary—nevertheless, precisely
then, I will trust the Lord who made me."*

❧ GEORGE EVERETT ROSS

Within the span of two and half years: my father died after suffering terribly from lumbar stenosis and heart problems; we sold the family home and moved my mother into a mobile home; after she fell and broke her hip we had to transfer her to a nursing facility where she died at age 90; eight months later my brother John died of cancer. In between these three deaths, I buried three aunts and an uncle. Then my brother Paul was diagnosed with cancer, my 42-year-old nephew had a heart attack, and my 3-year-old grandnephew suffered a stroke. As my friends consoled me, I found myself thinking, "I feel just like Job!"

The Book of Job is that classic story that probes the question: Why do the innocent suffer? Job is a good man, a faithful believer in God. He is also rich and prosperous. When God brags about Job's goodness to Satan, Satan says, "Easy for him to be a believer now! But if he weren't so prosperous, he wouldn't be such a believer." (That's a rather free translation.) God then permits bad things to happen to Job: He loses his flocks, his house, and even all his children. Finally Job himself is afflicted with a terrible, ugly disease. He is so miserable, his wife tells him, "Curse God and die!" But Job refuses to do either.

Job's friends conclude that he must have sinned grievously to have merited such suffering. But Job knows in his heart he has not. In his anguish, Job finally "has it out" with God. "How could you allow this to happen?" he cries. It is a question we too have probably asked God on more than one occasion. After listening to Job's lament, God finally speaks to Job—at length. He never answers Job's question or gives reasons for Job's sufferings. Instead he asks

Job a series of questions beginning with: "Where were you when I founded the earth?" Through God's questions, Job realizes how far beyond his comprehension God is. At the end, he surrenders his understanding to God, adding, "I had heard of you by word of mouth, but now my eye has seen you." Job realizes that his personal relationship with God, a relationship of love and trust, is far more important than the answer to his question, "Why?"

I draw comfort from Madeleine L'Engle's words: "Terrible things are not God's will, but God can enter them with redemptive love. That is the promise of the Incarnation." Like Job, we may never know why some terrible things befall us or our loved ones. Can we accept that? We can if we have a deep, personal relationship with God who says to us, "My ways are not always your ways. But trust me. Trust *me*."

Loving God,
it is easy for me to believe in you
    when things are going my way.
How much more difficult it is to believe in you
    when bad things befall me or those I love.
When I feel like Job and ask, "Why, God?"
    help me to remember that your ways are not
    always my ways.
And you yourself are far beyond my
    comprehension.
Give me the grace to love you and trust you
    during times of anguish as well as ecstasy.
    Amen.

Reflection

Do I ever feel like Job? What helps me get through such times?

Action

I will do one thing today to nourish my personal relationship with God.

22

Surrendering Control

*What the caterpillar calls the end, the
rest of the world calls a butterfly.*

❧ Lao-Tzu

Father Richard Rohr has said, "The essence of pain is when I am not in control." I think he's on to something there. I know many people who say, "I want to die before I become a burden to anyone." It sounds rather altruistic. *I do not want to be a burden to anyone else.* But if we look a little deeper at those words, what is really being said sometimes is this: "I want to die before I lose control." Lose control of what? Of anything—my arms, my legs, my decision making, my daily schedule, my bowels, my mind.

Losing control is so frightening some people pray to die "with their boots on," that is, to die in the midst of their normal activity. A sister in my community died while walking her third graders over to church, a friend while eating his breakfast, a cousin while buying a lottery ticket. But for many people, death comes after a period of surrendering control—sometimes a brief period, other times a lengthy one.

Surrendering control can be terrifying if all we see is what we are losing or leaving behind. But surrendering becomes easier if we see what we might be gaining or entering into. The lowly caterpillar can teach us a valuable lesson here. By surrendering its "caterpillar-ness" (i.e., its caterpillar stage), the caterpillar becomes a beautiful butterfly. The chrysalis, which looked like an end to life, was really the transformation into a brand new life.

Sometimes we freely surrender something for what we perceive as something better. For example, we surrender some of our free time for a friendship, one job for another one, four years of our life for a college education, and our single life for a spouse and children. Other times surrendering is imposed upon us: We lose our job, we need more nursing care, our spouse dies, we are faced with our own mortality. In these situations, the only thing we can hang on to is our trust in God, coupled with the conviction that what looks like evil may be good, what looks like loss may be gain, and what looks like death may be the transformation into new life.

Gerard Broccola, in his book *Vital Spiritualities,* writes: "The more I live the dregs and depths of life, the more I have come to believe in the 'God of the unraveled,' the God who is experienced not only when everything comes together, but also when everything falls apart. For this is truly the God beyond the projection of our own fantasies, the God who is truly other."

Almighty God,
I fear losing control.
I fear becoming a burden to anyone.
In many ways I would like to be in control until the
*   moment I die.*
But teach me the wisdom of surrendering.
Help me to surrender when I have no choice
*   and even sometimes when I do have a choice.*
Lead me to see that what looks like evil
*   may be good,*
what looks like loss
*   may be gain,*
and what looks like death
*   may be the transformation into new life.*
I ask for this grace through Jesus
*   who surrendered all on Calvary for love of us.*
*   Amen.*

✍ Reflection

I will reflect on a time when I had to surrender something. What loss was involved? Was there a gain? Is God asking me to surrender something at this time in my life?

✍ Action

I will surrender something today—even if it is only a grudge, a bad attitude, or a stubborn opinion.

23

Praying the Psalms during Troubled Times

The psalms help us get through those dark valleys of perplexity where God cannot be seen and his ways cannot be understood. — MARK D. FUTATO

In his book *Being Sick Well,* Jeffrey Boyd interviews people suffering with chronic illness. He elicits from them their strategies for coping with suffering. At the top of the list is prayer. But prayer doesn't always mean saying nice things to God in pretty words. On the contrary, when we are in pain, our prayer can be reduced to tears, cries, and wailings. That's one reason I love the psalms.

The psalms are ancient prayers that express the wide range of human emotion—from misery to ecstasy. They are characterized by raw honesty. I find it consoling that almost half of the psalms are laments. Take Psalm 22. It begins with this agonizing cry: "My God, my God, why have you forsaken me?" It continues, "O My God, I cry by day, but you do not answer; and by night, but find no rest." The psalmist goes on lamenting for 21 verses.

But with verse 22 comes a dramatic shift. The psalmist begins to speak of hope and trust in God. Verse 24 says, "God did not hide his face from me, but heard when I cried out." What is the cause of this shift? We don't know. Perhaps the very articulation of the pain was somehow cathartic. Or maybe there is a time gap between the lament and the praise. Whatever the cause, the fact remains: Psalm 22, which began in despair, ends in hope. Suffering has led to deeper trust in God.

Jesus himself prayed Psalm 22 as he hung dying on the cross. Even he felt abandoned by God. Yet, his final words on the cross (from Psalm 31) reveal his ultimate trust in Abba: "Father, into your hands I commend my spirit" (Luke 23:46). Jesus' suffering brought him to absolute trust in God.

When we are in pain, we might want to turn to the psalms of lament, starting with some of these: Psalms 3, 5, 6, 13, 23, 31, 38, 69, 70, 71, 86, 102. Psalms such as these remind us that suffering is not always something to be bypassed; sometimes it is something we must pass through to attain greater wholeness. In his book *The Book of Psalms Speaks Today,* Mark D. Futato, says it well: "The

Book of Psalms teaches us that...in the perplexity of doubt and fear and anger and confusion, God meets us. And in this meeting we are changed."

My God, help me to remember
   that prayer doesn't always mean saying nice
   things in pretty words.
That when I am in pain,
   my prayer can be reduced to tears, cries,
   and wailings.
Give me a greater love and appreciation
   for the psalms,
   especially the psalms of lament.
Like the psalmist, may I freely and honestly express
   my feelings to you,
   knowing that, in doing so,
I will meet you and be changed. Amen.

✍ Reflection

What are some of my favorite psalms and why?

✍ Action

I will pray a psalm of lament today.

24

Dealing with Setbacks

Everything that happens to you is your teacher. The secret is to learn to sit at the feet of your life and be taught.

                  — POLLY BERRIEN BERENDS

A few months after I started being treated for polymyositis, I had a setback. A "setback" is any stopping of forward progress. A really serious setback can actually be a reversal. I reacted to this setback with frustration, fear, and disappointment. "I was doing so well," I found myself saying. "And now this."

We seldom return to good health without a setback or two. We seldom reach a goal without a few snags or u-turns along the way.

We seldom make forward progress on any level without an occasional hitch or glitch. It behooves us then to reflect on how we deal with setbacks in our life—both small and large ones. Looking at Jesus can provide us with insights and inspiration.

Jesus' life did not run smoothly. In fact, on one level, his life was a whole series of setbacks. First of all, he was born in relative poverty. That fact in itself was a setback. He was raised in an insignificant little town that had produced no one of renown. Opportunities to get ahead were few for him—another setback. When he began his preaching, Jesus was a scandal to some members of his own family who thought he was crazy. He never won the respect of those in authority either. In fact, he antagonized them so much, they eventually wanted him dead. Throughout his life Jesus was misunderstood even by his own disciples. He was taunted and despised by certain religious leaders. Eventually Jesus was hunted down, arrested, and subjected to an unjust trial. In the end, he was deserted by his friends as he died an excruciating death, crucified between two common criminals. On one level, his death was just the final setback in a long string of setbacks that stretched from Bethlehem to Calvary.

Some of these setbacks must have been very difficult for Jesus, yet he eventually took all of them in stride. He didn't let any of them deter him from his mission. Why? Because Jesus knew that none of these setbacks could impede his forward progress in the one area of his life he considered absolutely essential: his personal relationship with God, his trust in Abba, his Father. The proof that this loving relationship endured despite all the setbacks, can be found in Jesus' prayer in Gethsemane when he submits his will to God's with these words: "Not my will but yours be done" (Luke 22:42). Facing the monumental setback of his crucifixion, Jesus fell back on the one "sure thing" he believed in: God's enduring love for him. Even death itself, therefore, proved to be no real setback for Jesus, for his final words on the cross were, "Father, into your hands I commend my spirit."

Jesus died "moving forward," that is, entrusting himself completely to Abba. We are called to do likewise.

Loving God,
I have known many setbacks in my life.
Some have been minor; others have been
*   major ones.*
Give me the patience to endure these setbacks
*   as I journey along life's road.*
Like Jesus, may I have the courage to make
*   forward progress*
in the one area of my life that is absolutely
*   essential:*
*   my personal relationship with you,*
*   my absolute trust in your love and goodness.*
When I encounter a setback that seems irreversible,
*   may I pray the words that Jesus prayed:*
*   Not my will but yours be done. Amen.*

✎ Reflection

What are some of the setbacks I have encountered in life? Did my trust in God help me to deal with them?

✎ Action

Today I will pray Jesus' words: Not my will but yours be done.

❧ 25 ❧

The Cross

The cross is a minus sign turned into a plus. ❧ Dr. Jacob Mathew

My Grandpa Svoboda died of congestive heart failure in 1943 at the age of 53. He died at home with his family keeping vigil with him. My Aunt Alice, a young woman at the time, said at one point, Grandpa suddenly reached up from his bed and touched the crucifix that hung on the wall behind him. He died shortly afterwards. Many years later when my Aunt Alice lost her husband, someone gave her a small crucifix to hold in her hand during the wake and funeral. She clutched that crucifix the whole time, telling me that just holding it gave her strength.

For millions of people, the cross has been a source of strength and consolation. This great symbol of Christianity, recognized all over the world, is a potent symbol. First, it reminds us how Jesus died. He was executed. We must never forget that. The cross also proclaims that suffering lies at the heart of the gospel—and indeed at the heart of our lives. Christianity doesn't promise to take suffering away. On the contrary, it says if we are truly Christian then we must (in Jesus' own words) take up our cross and follow Jesus. Christianity is not for sissies.

Jesus tells us that any authentic living of the gospel will, sooner or later, entail suffering. Why? Because *doing good* entails suffering, and the Gospel is essentially about doing good. As Cardinal John Henry Newman wrote, "No good is accomplished except at the cost of the one who performs the good."

The cross means much to me personally. When I was growing up we had a crucifix in almost every room of the house. Even today I admit I am a little dismayed when there is no cross anywhere in the home of people who are Christian. By law, every Catholic Church must have a crucifix. I believe that is highly significant as well as very right. And I for one always draw strength from making the sign of the cross.

As we face the trials of our daily lives, having a cross or crucifix nearby can be a source of comfort and strength. Recently a friend gave me a beautiful wooden cross about 4 inches long made of olive wood from the pruned branches of a tree in Jerusalem. Its edges are rounded and smooth, the grain rich and striking. The Printery House of Conception Abbey, which sells these crosses, calls them "comfort crosses." They are designed to be held in your hand.

The cross fits perfectly. It feels good, proper, right. There are times when my prayer is wordless, and I just sit clutching this precious piece of wood in my hand. It is one way of thanking Jesus for his sacrifice on the cross, while begging him to help me bear my crosses with greater courage and love.

Jesus,
for millions of people
> *the cross has been a source of strength and*
> *consolation.*
It is for me too.
Thank you for the terrible death you endured
> *out of love for all of us, including me.*
Thank you for reminding me
> *that you won't necessarily take my trials away,*
but you will always give me strength to bear them.
Help me to reverence your cross wherever I see it—
> *in my home,*
> *at church,*
> *or around someone's neck.*
I ask this (+) in the name of the Father
> *and of the Son*
> *and of the Holy Spirit. Amen.*

✍ Reflection

What does the cross mean for me personally? Is there a cross or crucifix in my home?

✍ Action

Today I will make the sign of the cross with greater reverence.

❧ 26 ❧

Paschal Deaths

Nothing is solid, everything moves.
Except love—hold on to love.

❧ Sister Helen Prejean

One day Jesus said to his disciples: "Very truly, I tell you, unless a grain of wheat falls into the earth and dies, it remains just a single grain; but if it dies, it bears much fruit" (John 12:24). These words of Jesus encapsulate what is called the Paschal Mystery. Jesus is saying that in order for us to come to the fullness of life, we must be willing to let go of our present life. In order to be born anew, we must first undergo death.

In his book *The Holy Longing,* Father Ronald Rolheiser distinguishes between two types of death: terminal death and paschal death. Terminal death, he writes, "ends life and ends all possibilities." But paschal death, "while ending one type of life, opens the person undergoing it to receive a richer form of life."

Paschal death is not a once-in-a-lifetime experience. Nor is it reserved for when we actually die. No, throughout our lives we can experience various kinds of paschal deaths. For example, if we live long enough, we will experience the paschal death of our youth. This death can be difficult because we live in a culture that glorifies youth. The boom in cosmetic surgery attests to this. Although there may be nothing inherently wrong with face lifts and tummy tucks, it is wrong to cling to our youth so tenaciously that we go into a tailspin over every new wrinkle or every lost hair. Or we keep wishing we were younger. Something is amiss when we do not accept our current age, because, after all, we are exactly the age God wants us to be. But if we accept the death of our youth as a paschal death, we will likely be more open to the blessings inherent in being older. Our faith says, "The God who gave you your youth will now give you life in a deeper way. Let go of your youth. Embrace being older." What a witness to the Paschal Mystery are people who can say, "It's good to be forty...fifty....sixty...seventy...eighty...ninety!"

Paschal death takes other forms as well. Sometimes we must die to our dreams, our good health, our idea of church, and even our understanding of God. Each death can be painful, but the new life that is bestowed is well worth the pain.

On Easter morning, Mary Magdalene meets the Risen Jesus near the tomb. Thinking he is the gardener she cries, "Sir, if you have carried him away, tell me where you have laid him, and I will take him" (John 20:15). Jesus says, "Mary," and instantly she recognizes him. She must have thrown her arms around him, for he says, "Do not hold on to me." Some translations say, "Stop clinging" or even "Stop choking me!" The incident shows that Mary must let go of the old Jesus, a Jesus who was familiar, touchable, and understandable. She must now be open to the new Jesus, risen in splendor and glory.

> *Risen Jesus,*
> *give me a greater appreciation of the*
> *Paschal Mystery.*
> *Help me to see that some deaths are not terminal,*
> *they are paschal, that is,*
> *they open me up to a richer and fuller life.*
> *Help me to let go of those things*
> *that I may be clinging to:*
> *my youth,*
> *my personal preferences,*
> *my stubborn opinions,*
> *my independence,*
> *my ideas of church,*
> *my understanding of you.*
> *I ask you for this grace, because I truly believe*
> *your words:*
> *if the grain of wheat dies,*
> *it will bring forth much fruit. Amen.*

🐦 Reflection

What have been some of the paschal deaths in my life? How did these deaths open me to a richer and fuller life?

🐦 Action

I will hear Jesus say to me today, "Stop clinging," and I will let go of whatever I need to let go of.

❧ 27 ❧

The Eucharist and Suffering

The truly amazing aspect of our gathering for the Eucharist is this: as imperfect as we all are, Jesus chooses to make his home in us.

❧ Sister Melannie Svoboda, SND

In the latter part of the tenth century, Vladimir, the Prince of Kiev, sent envoys to various Christian churches to study their worship services. This is what his envoys reported after witnessing the celebration of the Eucharist at the Great Church of Holy Wisdom in Constantinople: "We knew not whether we were in heaven or on earth, for surely there is no such splendor or beauty anywhere on earth. We cannot describe it to you; we only know that God dwells there among (the people)."

Some might be thinking: those words don't describe the celebration of the Eucharist at *my* parish—with people scooting in late, babies fussing, and a sound system that doesn't always work. But whatever the external reality of our worship service, the fact remains: In our celebration of the Eucharist, God does indeed dwell among us—the people—in a special way. When we are experiencing pain, the Eucharist is especially important for us as sacrifice and meal.

The Eucharist is a sacrifice, rooted in the passion and death of Jesus. When we celebrate the Eucharist, then, we are uniting our sufferings with the sufferings of Jesus. *The Catechism of the Catholic Church* says, "In the Eucharist the sacrifice of Christ becomes also the sacrifice of the members of his Body. The lives of the faithful, their praise, their sufferings, prayer, and work are united with those of Christ and his total offering, and so acquire new value" (no. 1368).

But our celebration is more than a remembrance of Good Friday. Pope John Paul II reminded us that every celebration of the Eucharist makes present "the events of the paschal mystery of Jesus' suffering, death, and resurrection." All three. Father Bernard Bourgeois describes this amazing truth in this way: "At one and the same time, the person [who celebrates the Eucharist] is sacramentally in the upper room of the Last Supper, nailed to the cross with Christ, and standing in awe and wonder at the empty tomb." When we are in pain, we may feel nailed to the cross, but little else.

Even then we can take hope in the realization that we are simultaneously standing before that empty tomb—although for now, we may be able to experience that only by faith.

The Eucharist is also a meal in which we receive the body and blood of Christ. It is our spiritual nourishment for our journey of faith. When we are in pain, we need the Eucharist more than ever. Among my cherished memories are those times I took my elderly parents to Mass. They would hobble up the main aisle to the front pew with their cane or walker, smiling and nodding to their friends along the way. I sensed just being in their familiar parish church gave them strength to bear the sufferings associated with aging. When my parents were too ill to go to church, I would take them communion. What a privilege it was for me to place the sacred host in their gnarled hands and say those sacred words, "The Body of Christ."

Loving Jesus,
I thank you for your suffering, death, and
    resurrection,
which are made present
    in every celebration of the Eucharist.
Help me to see beneath the surface
    of the celebration to the deepest reality:
    In the Eucharist you choose to make
       your home in us.
Help me to unite my prayer, sufferings,
    works, and joys with yours.
Give me the spiritual nourishment I need
    to continue my journey of faith with love,
    courage, and hope. Amen.

Reflection

What does the Eucharist mean to me? How can I participate in the celebration of the Eucharist with greater love?

Action

Is there someone I could bring to Mass or ask to take me to Mass? Or is there someone to whom I could bring communion—or someone I could ask to bring me communion?

❧ 28 ❧

Responding to the Pain of Others

We can't build a good society on the principles of self-interest and entitlement alone. Without generosity, there can be no community. ❧ SAM KEEN

We Christians are called to do more than ponder our sufferings and unite them with those of Jesus Christ. We are called to alleviate the suffering of others. Jesus' parable of the last judgment makes this absolutely clear: We will be judged on how we respond to those in pain, that is, the hungry, the thirsty, the stranger, the naked, the ill, and the imprisoned

(Matthew 25:31–46). This call to alleviate the suffering of others is not an option. It is a mandate. No excuses will be accepted.

The seriousness of this mandate is glimpsed in an incident in the life of St. Jerome. St. Jerome was a scholar noted for translating the Bible and writing theological works. But when refugees flooded his area after the sacking of Rome in 404, he left his writing and studies to help with the refugees. He wrote, "I cannot help them all, but I grieve and weep with them, and am completely absorbed in the duties that charity imposes on me." He put aside his translating, saying, "Today we must translate the precepts of the Scriptures into deeds. Instead of speaking saintly words, we must act them."

We too will be called to put aside even good works in order to help someone in need or in pain. Parents do this every time they help their children, spouses every time they assist their spouses. This reaching out can extend to an elderly parent, a lonely neighbor, a sick friend, a troubled coworker. We respond in various ways: by expressing our genuine concern for them, running errands, preparing meals, visiting them, or praying with and for them. We can join our efforts to those of our parish community or local community. Collecting clothing or toys, for example, or packing food for distribution at a food bank are ways we extend Jesus' compassion in our time and place. Reaching out to those in pain also includes becoming more involved in political, economic, and social issues. We can educate ourselves about a vital topic, join a local discussion group, or write a letter to our representatives in Congress. The needs are so great and the issues are so complex, we may be tempted to think, "What can one person do?" But the fact remains, although we cannot do everything, we can do at least one thing. Find that one thing.

When we read about wars and violence in our world, when we see pictures of malnourished babies and people dying of AIDS, or when we see images of the effects of natural disasters such as hurricanes and earthquakes, we are quick to ask, "Why? Why?" But the most important question to ask is not "Why?" It is, "How can I help?"

Compassionate Jesus,
you gave us the mandate to alleviate the
suffering of others.
You told us to reach out to the hungry,
the thirsty, the stranger,
the naked, the ill, the imprisoned.
Help me to reach out to those in pain—
family members, friends, neighbors,
and even total strangers.
Teach me to join my efforts with those of others,
to take actions concerning political, economic,
and social issues.
Although I cannot do everything,
I can do at least one thing.
Help me to find that one thing.
When disasters strike and I cry out, "Why? Why?"
remind me to ask the more important question:
How can I help? Amen.

❧ Reflection

What are some of the ways I already try to alleviate the pain of others? What more might God be calling me to do?

❧ Action

I will reach out to one person in pain today.

❧ 29 ❧

Chairs for
My Company

God walks in when we're loving.

❧ JOHN POWELL, SJ

As my mother lay dying in the nursing home, her children, grandchildren, and great-grandchildren gathered around her bed for the last time. Mom was very alert. No matter how weak she was, she always perked up when visitors came. At one point there were so many of us in the room, several of us had to stand. Seeing this, Mom motioned me over and whispered in my ear, "Can we find more chairs for my company?" A little while later she asked me, "Do you think we can find some food for my guests?"

My mother amazed me. Here she was dying, and yet she was still thinking of others. Perhaps I shouldn't have been so surprised though, for Mom had been the consummate hostess her entire life. Who could begin to count the number of guests she had served in her home over the years? Mom died as she had lived: thinking of others. She was still serving them to the end.

Sometimes when we are ill or in pain, we assume our condition excuses us from thinking of others or from serving them. But that's not true. We are never excused from the great commandment of loving. But when we are ill or in pain, our service may take a different form.

One of our sisters, Sister Elreda, lived to be ninety-seven. The last few years of her life she was confined to a wheelchair and bed. From one perspective, she could do nothing. Everything had to be done for her. If anyone could be excused from thinking about others, it would have been she. But at her wake, a woman who did the housekeeping in our health care center got up and went to the microphone to say a few words about Sister. She said something like this: "Every time I came into Sister Elreda's room to clean, she greeted me with a big smile. She always asked about me and my family. And she always promised to pray for them. And every time I left, she thanked me for cleaning her room." Sister Elreda, as helpless and infirm as she was, was thinking of others. She served the people who came into her room with her warm greeting, her interest in them, her prayers, and her gratitude.

No matter how intense our pain or how serious our illness, we can still serve others with a smile, a prayer, and a "thank you." As Mother Teresa said, we are called not to do great things; rather we are called to do "small things with great love."

Loving God,
I ask for the grace to live your commandment
   of love
   on good days as well as bad days,
when I am eager and when I am reluctant,
   when I am healthy and when I am ill.
May I serve others all the days of my life
   if only with a smile, a prayer, and a "thank you."
Help me to do small things with great love.
I ask for this grace through Jesus,
   who served all of us all the way to Calvary.
   Amen.

Reflection

What are some of the forms my service of others
has taken during my life?

Action

Today I will serve someone in need.

30

Biblical Images of Pain and Suffering

The universe is not made up of atoms,
but of stories. ➮ MURIEL RUKEYSER

The Bible is filled with gripping images of pain and suffering. These images can give us insight and encouragement as we navigate the stormy seas of life. In this chapter, we will explore three images of pain from scripture: a woman in labor, an athlete working out, and an estranged father and son reuniting.

The first image of pain comes from Jesus' discourse at the Last Supper where he compares his impending passion and death to a woman in labor. He says, "When a woman is in labor, she has pain, because her hour has come. But when her child is born, she no longer remembers the anguish because of the joy of having brought a human being into the world" (John 16:21). This image tells us that our pain, no matter how intense, is only temporary. What's more, it can bring forth new life. This means that our earthly suffering will probably look very different from the perspective of eternity. St. Teresa of Avila supposedly said that, from heaven, the most miserable earthly life will look like one bad night in a cheap hotel.

In his first letter to the Corinthians, St. Paul gives us another image of pain that probably appealed to the sports-loving Greeks. Paul compares discipleship with being an athlete—more specially, a runner or a boxer. Paul writes, "Athletes exercise self-control in all things... " (1 Corinthians 9:25). We know athletes train vigorously for their competitions, pushing their bodies to the limit while subscribing to the motto "No pain, no gain." Why do they do this? For "a perishable crown"—a laurel leaf, a medal, a trophy, a ring. Paul tells the Corinthians, "do not run aimlessly..." "run in such a way that you may win" (1 Corinthians 9:26, 24). In other words, if athletes endure pain for a mere temporal prize, how much more can we put up with pain—especially the pain of discipleship—for an eternal prize, life everlasting.

The third image comes from the parable of the Prodigal Son. There is a lot of pain in this story, most notably that of the father and the younger son. The father's pain is essentially threefold: His younger son is ungrateful, he has gone away, and the father is worried sick about him. This pain drives the father to watch for his son's return every day. He is a man full of hope and he is eager to forgive. The younger son's pain stems largely from his destitution and his shame. This pain drives him to say, "I will get up and go to my father" (Luke 15:18). The pain of these two main characters moves them to action—and to one another. Pain compels the son to return and beg forgiveness. Pain compels the father to watch for, run toward, embrace, and forgive. In both instances, pain was the impetus for reconciliation.

These biblical images give us additional ways to view our pain: as birth pangs bringing forth new life, as the consequence of our discipleship, and as the impetus for action that leads to reconciliation.

> *Jesus, you compared the pain of your passion*
> >   *and death*
> >   *to that of a woman in labor.*
> *This rich image seemed to give you courage*
> >   *for it reminded you that your agony would be*
> >   *temporary,*
> *and it would bring forth new life not only for you*
> >   *but for all of us.*
> *Help me to view the pain and suffering in my life*
> >   *with new eyes.*
> *Help me to see that some of my pain is birth pangs.*
> *Some is the consequence of my discipleship.*
> *And still other pain may be the impetus I need*
> >   *to take action that leads to reconciliation.*

May I always remember that all earthly pain
will pale
in comparison to the heavenly joys
awaiting us in eternity. Amen.

✍ Reflection

Which image of pain speaks most to me at this time in my life? Are there other biblical images of pain that speak to me as well?

✍ Action

I will ask Jesus to help me view pain and suffering in new, life-giving ways.

❧ 31 ❧

Sister Cora

*There are two things God endlessly
communicates to us: I am with you. And
the way I am with you is love.*

❧ PATRICIA LIVINGSTON

I sat with Sister Cora in a parlor in our health care center. It was a cold, wet December day. A small gentle woman, Sister had agreed to talk with me about her cancer—her surgeries, radiation treatments, and pain. First, some background.

Four years ago, at age sixty-six, Sister Cora learned she had uterine cancer. She had a complete hysterectomy. A few months later, the cancer had spread. She endured twenty-eight radiation treatments in five "spots" followed by three radiation implants. "The pain was pretty bad," she said softly. Ten months later, the cancer was back. This time she had twenty-five radiation treatments in five spots and three more implants. The side effects of the radiation were terrible: blisters, a series of blood clots, and a hideous burn that caused even a veteran nurse to gasp. The day we spoke, Sister was awaiting more tests. Because of the way she felt, she suspected the cancer might be back.

"How did you get through four years of this?" I asked. "What sustained you?"

She was quick to reply: "The prayers and support of others—especially the nuns and the parish community where I worked. Their cards, emails, and hugs sustained me."

I asked her about her prayer—especially when the pain was at its worst. She said, "I couldn't pray during that time. Not at all." She said she felt she was in a "dark tunnel" where God seemed far away or even non-existent.

"What did you do?" I asked.

She said, "I read mystery novels." And we both smiled.

These books got her mind off her pain—at least for a while. At first she felt guilty for not praying until a nun friend said to her, "Don't worry. We, your sisters, will do your praying for you during this time."

Later, it was the image of God as Father that helped sustain her. As a child, Sister feared the dentist, so her father would take her by the hand and gently lead her to the door of the dentist's office. Now, many years later, she said, "When I would get out of my car to go in for another radiation treatment, I would stand there for a few minutes and, in my mind, I would take God the Father's hand

and walk into the building. Some days that image was the only thing that got me to go back into that building."

Small acts of kindness meant much to her as well. One evening two nuns "kidnapped" her from the health care center and took her out for ice cream. Another friend brought her books to read. "Besides the pain," I said, "what's been the hardest part of these past four years?" She said, "The cancer has taken away the world I knew. I had to say goodbye to all my plans." I asked, "What's been the best part of these four years?" She said, "I no longer fear tomorrow, because I know my Heavenly Father is already there waiting for me."

Heavenly Father, Heavenly Mother,
    be with me in my pain.
Give me a deep sense of your presence
    even when I feel I'm in a dark tunnel.
Give me family and friends who will help
    sustain me
    with their love and prayers.
May I be open to their support
    and to any small kindnesses they may wish to
    show me.
If I can't pray, assure me that it's okay
    not to pray for now,
    that my suffering itself may be my prayer.
I ask these things through Jesus,
    who suffered, died, and rose
out of love for all humanity—including me. Amen.

✿ Reflection

What struck me the most in Sister Cora's story?
Why?

✿ Action

I will support someone in pain today—by a note, a
small kindness, or a prayer.

32

Leading a Listening Life

Lead a listening life. Order your outward life so that nothing drowns out the listening. ❧ THOMAS KELLY

In responding to our own pain and the pain of others, we need to recognize the critical importance of listening. This listening is two-sided. First, we must listen to the articulation of our own pain. Second, we must listen to the articulation of the pain of others.

When we ourselves are in pain, we must first acknowledge our pain. We must never deny or downplay it. Saying things like, "I'm fine," when we're in agony or "It's nothing," when our world is falling apart, serves us no good. It is important to express our pain to someone—a doctor or nurse, yes, but also a trusted friend or family member, and of course God. Why is this so important? Father James Keenan, SJ, professor of moral theology at Weston Jesuit School of Theology, explains it this way: "In suffering, we face the loss of our own personal universe. In order to claim a new universe, the suffering need to articulate the fears, hopes, and concerns that they have."

In scripture, God is often depicted as a good listener. When Job was in agony, for example, he turns to God in prayer. At first God is silent. But it is a listening silence that elicits from Job a lengthy lament about his pain and suffering. This lament proves to be a critical step in Job's healing process.

When we listen to someone expressing pain we must really listen. This means we never minimize their pain. The spiritual writer Father Benedict Groeschel, CFR, says rightly, "There must be a special place in purgatory for people who tell the suffering, 'Cheer up. It's not so bad.'" We also have to fight the urge to interpret people's pain. We do not say things like this: "If you had taken better care of your health, this wouldn't have happened to you," or "God sent you this suffering because God loves you very much."

Listening to someone in pain is not only beneficial to the one who is suffering, it can also be transformative for the one who listens. Sometimes this transformation is dramatic. Jean Donovan, a lay woman, volunteered for the Cleveland mission in El Slavador to minister to the people suffering from abject poverty and a bloody civil war. She was dramatically transformed as she listened to the stories of the people she served. Her listening convinced her to stand in solidarity with them. She knew, by doing so, her own life was in danger. She wrote to a friend explaining her decision: "Several times I have decided to leave El Salvador. I almost could except for the children, the poor, the bruised victims of this insanity. Who would care for them? Whose heart could be as staunch as to favor the reasonable thing in a sea of their tears and loneliness? Not mine, dear friend, not mine." Jean Donovan decided to stand with the people. It was a decision that cost her her life.

> *Listening God,*
> *teach me the art of listening.*
> *Help me to listen to myself as I articulate*
>   *my sufferings.*
> *Help me also to listen to others as they tell me*
>   *of their pain.*
> *May I never minimize another's pain,*
>   *interpret it for them, or explain it away.*
> *By listening to the pain of others,*
>   *may I be transformed into a more loving*
>   *and compassionate person,*
> *like Jesus, your Son. Amen.*

✍ Reflection

Have I ever listened well to someone expressing his or her pain? What effect did my listening have on the other person and on me?

✍ Action

I will listen attentively to someone in pain today.

❧ 33 ❧

Being Strong Isn't Everything

Where God guides, God provides.

❧ FRANK BUCHMAN

B eing strong isn't everything. Ask St. Paul. In his second letter to the Corinthians, he described a problem that caused him great anguish. He wrote: "A thorn in the flesh was given to me, an angel of Satan, to beat me, to keep me from being too elated" (2 Corinthians 12:8). What exactly was Paul's "thorn in the flesh"? No one knows for sure. Some speculate that it was a chronic physical ailment. Others say it was some kind of deep psychological problem or a grave temptation. Whatever it was, Paul, as resourceful and strong as he was, was powerless to do anything about it. So he begged God for relief, for a cure. But God didn't take away Paul's problem. Instead God said to him, "My grace is sufficient for you, for power is made perfect in weakness" (2 Corinthians 12:9).

Like Paul, we too experience the pain of human weakness in a variety of ways: a chronic bodily ailment, the inability to live up to our ideals, a personality problem, persistent fatigue, jealousies, physical diminishment, laziness, forgetfulness, debilitating fears. Like St. Paul, we too may beg God to relieve us of our weakness. But if that doesn't happen, then perhaps St. Paul's words can give us encouragement.

For St. Paul says his weakness is a good thing, for it provides a better opportunity for God's power to work in him than his own recovery would. Rather than boasting of his own strength, St. Paul boasts of God's strength working in him. He concludes with this fundamental paradox of our faith: "I am content with weakness, insults, hardships, persecutions, and calamities for the sake of Christ; for whenever I am weak, then I am strong" (2 Corinthians 8:10).

If our prayers for relief from a nagging situation seem to go unanswered, it does not mean that God is ignoring our prayers. It might mean that God is providing us with a greater strength than our own: God's own strength to endure the difficult circumstances. This strength of God can work wonders in us. Perhaps it gives us the ability to accept our condition with cheerfulness. Or it might give us greater humility to allow others to help or care for us, extra patience with the weaknesses of others, or deeper compassion for those who suffer in similar ways.

Cardinal John Henry Newman expressed the potential link between our weakness and our love for others when he wrote, "Taught by our own pain, our own sorrow, nay, by our own sin, we shall have hearts and minds exercised for every service of love toward those who need it."

> *Provident God,*
> *I want to be strong. I don't want to be weak.*
> *Like St. Paul, I often beg you*
> *to remove my weaknesses or the problems in*
> *my life.*
> *But, also like St. Paul, I sometimes hear you say,*
> *"My grace is sufficient for you."*
> *Help me to really believe those words.*
> *When I experience weakness, insults,*
> *hardships, persecutions, and constraints,*
> *give me the grace to rely on your power*
> *instead of my own.*
> *Lead me to see that being strong isn't everything.*
> *But being united with you by faith and love is!*
> *Amen.*

✸ Reflection

What weaknesses or problems am I struggling with right now? How do I feel God's strength upholding me?

✸ Action

I will ask for God's strength to bear my weaknesses today. And I will be patient with the weaknesses of others.

❧ 34 ❧

Sympathy Cards and the Resurrection

Christianity is a religion of the open tomb.
❧ ROY L. SMITH

Whenever I buy a sympathy card for someone, I come across cards that say things like this: "Know that your loved one lives on in your memories" or "May the support of your friends be your consolation during this time of loss." As nice as these sentiments are, they fall far short of what I, as a Christian, want to say to someone who has just lost a loved one. I want to say, "Know that your loved one lives on—and not merely in your memories!" And, "Yes, may the support of your friends be a consolation for you, but may your greatest consolation be the fact that Jesus rose from the dead—and he takes us with him!" For the cornerstone of our Christian faith is our belief in that empty tomb, a belief that profoundly influences our view of death.

The way I see it, either Jesus rose from the dead as all four gospels proclaim or he didn't. If he didn't, then he may have been a very nice man who said some very lovely things and died a tragic death, but that's about it. But if he did indeed rise from the dead, then this incredible event changes forever the way we look at death (and sympathy cards)—and the way we look at pain and suffering.

Jesus' resurrection says this to us: Death is not an end; it is a transition. Death is not the final act before oblivion; it is the first step into a whole new life, eternal life. Therefore, we do not bid our dying loved ones a *final* farewell. Instead we say things like this: "Goodbye—for now... I will see you again...We will be reunited someday soon." This view of death spills over onto the way we view pain and suffering too. We believe no pain is the end. No suffering is forever. They are only temporary. They are transitional. They too will evolve into new life.

The writer John Shea has written some beautiful poems about death that reflect this true Christian attitude. In one poem he describes heaven as a place where "the laughter of reunion leaps / on the far side of loss." I love that line, for it implies that heaven is one immense reunion with our loved ones, a reunion characterized by laughter and jubilation. In another poem, Shea writes these lines: "The partings that paralyze us, / the leavetakings that leave only ache, /...Shall Be No More!" Imagine, no more paralyzing partings, no more aching goodbyes!

I have found sympathy cards that express well my belief as a Christian. A card I sent recently said this: "May you find comfort in warm memories of the beautiful life that has passed. May you find peace in the assurance that an even more beautiful life has begun for your loved one." Jesus rose! We will rise too! Amen to that!

Jesus, I believe you rose from the dead.
But sometimes I take this earth-shaking event
*   for granted.*
Help me to see the tremendous implications
*   your resurrection*
*   has upon my view of life and death.*
Give me eyes to see that death is not an end,
*   but a transition;*
it is not a final parting,
*   but a temporary separation.*
Give me eyes also to see that pain and suffering
*   are transitional too.*
They also can lead to a new and greater life.
I ask these things of you, because I believe
*   you are indeed the God of the empty tomb.*
*   Amen.*

Reflection

How does my belief in the resurrection of Jesus impact my view of death, pain, and suffering?

Action

Today I will comfort someone who is mourning by my words, actions, prayers, or presence.

❧ 35 ❧

The Extraordinary Community of Goodness

Rain does not fall on one roof alone.

❧ CAMEROONIAN PROVERB

Scientist Carl Sagan contracted a rare blood disease in 1994 and lived until late 1996. One of the discoveries he made during his illness was "the extraordinary community of goodness" to which he said he owed his life. Sagan, a non-believer for most of his life, wrote, "When too much cynicism threatens to engulf us, it is good to remember how pervasive goodness is." He then told of five thousand people praying for him at a cathedral in

New York City, a large prayer vigil held for him on the banks of the Ganges, and Muslims and Jews writing to him promising their prayers for him.

When we are suffering, it is essential that we stay connected to this "extraordinary community of goodness." Such a task is not always easy, for illness and pain have a way of separating us from others. When we are suffering from depression, for example, our natural inclination is often to withdraw from people. When we are homebound by illness or old age, we may find ourselves cut off from family and friends. The problem is that pain and suffering are frequently intensified by isolation, whereas they are often assuaged by community.

Sara Dougherty, a Seattle exercise physiologist, has studied heart disease and its relationship to community. She writes, "Isolation is the most common shared contributor to heart disease. No education with respect to diet, stress, or exercise can compare to the healing value of community." In other words, interacting with other people is one of the best cardiovascular exercises available.

What are some of the ways we can stay connected to community? We can begin by making time for our old friends. A short visit, a phone call, a little note can work wonders—whether we're on the giving or receiving end. We can also be open to new friendships regardless of our age or physical condition. When my mother moved into a mobile home park at age eighty-seven, she met several new neighbors who soon became very good friends of hers.

We stay connected to community by keeping informed about what's happening in the local, national, and world communities; by joining a group like a book club or Bible study group; by taking a class at the local community center; by attending community events such as a parish picnic, the county fair, a concert, a play, or a baseball game; and by becoming more involved in our parish or diocese.

For us Christians, community is not an option. It is absolutely essential for our spiritual well-being.

> *God, you call us all to community.*
> *Help me to stay connected*
> > *to the "extraordinary community of goodness"*
> > *that surrounds me and to which I belong.*
> *When pain or illness tempts to isolate me*
> > *from others*
> *help me to find creative ways*
> > *to stay connected to family and friends.*
> *Give me the courage to reach out*
> > *to those in pain.*
> *And when I am in pain,*
> > *give me the courage to reach out to others*
> > *for help.*
> *Give me a deep experience of the healing power*
> > *of community.*
> *I ask for these graces through Jesus, who said,*
> > *"Where two or three are gathered in my name,*
> > *there am I in their midst." Amen.*

✑ Reflection

Have I ever experienced the "extraordinary community of goodness"? If so, when and how?

✑ Action

I will reach out to someone today—either someone I can help or someone who can help me.

❧ 36 ❧

Grief: The Cost of Loving

The risk of love is loss, and the price of loss is grief. But the pain of grief is only a shadow when compared to the pain of never loving. ❧ HILARY STANTON ZUNIN

I was sitting at the drive-thru window at the bank when my car radio started playing Franz von Suppe's "Poet and Peasant Overture." Instantly my eyes filled with tears. It took my brain several seconds to compute what was happening to me. "Poet and Peasant" was one of my deceased father's favorite classical pieces. He played it over and over again when I was growing up. Just hearing the opening strains of that beautiful piece brought tears to my eyes. Although my father had been dead for almost a year, my tears confirmed how much I still missed him and how much I was still grieving his loss.

The pain of grief is very real. Sometimes it is piercing, other times more subtle. Sometimes grief is fleeting, other times it lingers. At times we know what triggers the pain of grief: a photograph, a particular song, a certain place, a family get-together. Other times the pain comes out of nowhere and we are taken aback by our flood of tears or our sense of overwhelming sadness.

In the novel *The Poisonwood Bible*, by Barbara Kingsolver, a mother loses her young daughter. She describes her grief in this way: "As long as I kept moving, my grief streamed out behind me like a swimmer's long hair in water...Only when I stopped did the slick, dark stuff of it come floating around my face, catching my arms and throat till I began to drown....The substance of grief is not imaginary. It's as real as rope or the absence of air."

Why is grief so painful? Why, for some, does it last so long? Psychologists tell us that grieving is really a process of relearning the world. When a significant loved one dies, we must learn how to live in a new world, a world now void of their physical presence. This relearning means we must renegotiate our place in space and time. Little wonder grief can be so disconcerting. Little wonder it can take so much time. In fact, there are some people who would agree with the main character in Wendell Berry's novel, *Jaber Crow*, when he says this about grief: "I don't believe that grief passes away. It has its time and place forever... Grief and griever alike endure."

Grief cannot be rushed, nor should it be skirted. Rather, grief is something we must patiently allow ourselves to pass through. Psychologist Sister Donna Markham, OP, says that if we open ourselves to the grieving process, we also open ourselves "to the transformative power of emphatic love and compassion." In this way, grief can truly be a blessing.

Loving God,
the pain of grief is very real for me,
  sometimes subtle, other times intense.
Be with me in my grieving,
  whether I mourn the loss of a loved one
  or the loss of something else:
    my health,
    a job,
    a cherished idea,
    a favorite place,
    my youth,
    my independence,
    a dream.
Let me never be ashamed of my tears for a
  lost loved one,
  for my tears are the price I pay for loving them.

Give me patience to pass through the
grieving process,
knowing that grieving has the transformative
power
of emphatic love and compassion.
I ask for these graces through Jesus,
who wept bitterly at the death of his good friend,
Lazarus. Amen.

Reflection

What has been my experience of grief? Am I mourning anyone or anything at this time?

Action

I will be sensitive to everyone I meet today, knowing they are all grieving someone or something.

❧ Index ❧

(The number indicates the number of the reflection.)